Faith Development in Early Childhood

Edited by Doris A. Blazer

James W. Fowler   Kevin J. Swick

Alice S. Honig   Patricia J. Boone

Bettye M. Caldwell   Robert A. Boone

Lucie W. Barber

Sheed & Ward

Sheed & Ward™ is a service of National Catholic Reporter Publishing
Company, Inc.

Library of Congress Catalog Card Number: 88-61855

ISBN: 1-55612-212-8

Published by: Sheed & Ward
               115 E. Armour Blvd., P.O. Box 419492
               Kansas City, MO 64141

To order, call: (800) 333-7373

Contents

Introduction

God our Father, you see your children growing up in an unsteady
and confusing world; Show them that your ways give more life
than the ways of the world, and that following you is better than
chasing after selfish goals. Help them to take failure, not as a
measure of their worth, but as a chance for a new start. Give them
strength to hold their faith in you, and to keep alive their joy in
your creation; through Jesus Christ our Lord.

AMEN

These familiar words from *The Book of Common Prayer* (829) capture
both the reality and the hope of Christians everywhere. Indeed, the world
is unsteady and confusing. The unprecedented explosion of knowledge
and change during the past two decades has brought about great concern
for the fragility of the environment, the effects of chemical addiction and
sexually transmitted diseases, and the morality of decisions necessitated by
the development of life-altering technology. Man's inability to overcome
the mistrust and competitiveness which divides brothers and sisters is evi-
denced by intolerance of those who differ in color or creed, exploitative
relationships, soaring rates of violence against others' property and persons, acts of senseless terrorism, and the omnipresent threat of nuclear
warfare and potential annihilation of the human race. And when those
who offer leadership prove to be chasing after the selfish goals of material
wealth, power, or pleasure, it becomes increasingly difficult to help children develop a sense of joy in the goodness of God's creation.

Although these problems loom insurmountably large and menacing,
Christians throughout history have always believed in the power of the

Gospel to change people, and in the commitment of a community of changed people to bring about a more just, peaceful, and compassionate world. The proud proclamation of America's coinage, In God We Trust, continues to affirm that hope. The most recent Gallup Report on the role of religion in America found the overwhelming majority of its national sample believes in the concept of a personal God who hears prayers (84 percent) and who holds a specific plan for their lives (87 percent). And in repeated polling since 1980, seven out of ten claimed membership in a church or synagogue (although the number attending is more nearly four out of ten on any given Sunday); and six out of ten said that religion is important or very important in their own lives.

Such evidence of wide-spread commitment to religion as a basis for personal and societal decision-making brings hope to those who rear children in this unsteady world. While most Christian parents realize their power to bring a child into the world and protect it with love, they also recognize the importance of a safe and benevolent environment which will support their efforts toward full development of the child's God-given potential. For many young parents whose institutional religious commitment has faltered during early adulthood, the birth of their first child provides the impetus to seek a faith community which offers such support through programs of nurture and religious education. This high level of parental trust has resulted in churches becoming the single greatest institutional influence on preschool children in America since for every child who attends Sunday School, eight children daily come to the church for daycare, preschool, or some form of early childhood education and care (ECCN *Newsletter* 5). And another million school-age children are enrolled in church-sponsored elementary and high schools (Robinson).

These enrollments clearly indicate that faith communities have an unprecedented opportunity to influence the religious and moral development of millions of youngsters who may one day contribute to the resolution of this nation's problems. Unfortunately, exposure to religious and moral training carries no guarantees, as shown by data from a recent comprehensive sociological study involving the attitudes and behaviors of more than 8000 youngsters in grades five to nine, drawn from thirteen national churches and youth-service organizations, as they began the process of making moral choices independent of parental control. These youngsters were unusually well "churched;" compared to recent Gallup poll respondents, their 10,000 parents ranked very high on measures of religious commitment, with 98 percent of the mothers and 96 percent of the fathers attending services every week. Parental goals also indicated that 68 percent thought it was very important to help their children grow in religious faith, and 70 percent sought to help their children develop healthy concepts of right and wrong (Strommen and Strommen, 104-128).

Although the findings of this study are generally optimistic and helpful for guiding young adolescents, some trends which concern parents and religious educators are also identified. Not surprisingly, youngsters' responses revealed a steady decline in relying upon parents for guidance, down from 57 percent of the fifth graders to 21 percent of the ninth graders. In addition, as these youngsters claimed independence, they began turning to peers and questioning the religious beliefs which their parents valued and had tried to teach them. By the ninth grade only 38 percent replied that their church or synagogue helped them answer important questions about school or life, and the number of boys expressing religious doubts increased by a third, from 45 percent of the fifth graders to 62 percent of the ninth graders. Corresponding figures for the girls were somewhat lower: 42 percent of the fifth graders to 54 percent of the ninth graders (Strommen and Strommen, 104-128).

Of greater concern was the incongruence between these youngsters' professed beliefs and several behaviors which concern those who work with young adolescents. When asked about the use of alcoholic beverages, 61 percent of the ninth grade boys and 70 percent of the ninth grade girls replied it was wrong for Junior High students to drink alcohol; yet more than half revealed they had already done so. With regard to traditional religious teachings about sexual behaviors, 36 percent of the ninth grade boys and 61 percent of the ninth grade girls indicated they believed premarital intercourse was wrong; yet one in five ninth graders, including twice as many boys as girls, had already experienced sexual intercourse (Forliti and Benson, 212-213).

Psychologists of early adolescent growth and development interpret these findings as manifestations of the move toward personal identity and independence. However, that does not mean that early entry into alcohol usage and/or sexual activity should be an expected or acceptable part of the move to maturity. Nationally the consequences for these two behaviors are simply too high to be tolerated. Substance abuse has now become the leading cause of death in the teenage years, with half of all automobile accidents and homicides and a fourth of all suicides linked to its use. There are over a million teenage alcoholics in America today, with their average age of first drink being 12.6 years. Though the emotional pain to individuals and families cannot be measured, the cost of alcoholism to society now approaches more than $116 billion each year (Gallup, 3-5).

The outcomes of early entry into sexual activity are surely as well publicized among teenagers as the consequences of abusing alcohol. Out of the 11 million sexually active adolescent girls in this country, more than a million become pregnant each year, with 125,000 girls being under the age of fifteen. In 1985 half a million babies were born to teen mothers at a cost to the public of $1.4 billion. Because of immature reproductive systems and inadequate prenatal care, these young mothers' babies are three times more likely to require intensive medical care or to die in the first year of life. And the costs for the mother are life-long; only half of the adolescents who become mothers before the age of eighteen graduate from high school, and their lifetime earnings average only half those of a woman who waits until age twenty to bear a child (Edelman, 51-57).

Societal influences which cause youngsters to ignore church and family teachings and to risk the devastating consequences of premature entry into such behaviors as alcohol use and sexual activity have been well described by David Elkind, Neil Postman, and other contemporary social critics. Parents have begun to recognize the destructive effects of various kinds of media programming and advertising on their children's developing values and have formed advocacy groups such as the Washington-based Parents Music Resource Center (Gore). Faith communities are also becoming increasingly aware of the need to combat cultural messages of materialism, hedonism, racism, and glorified violence; and many denominational publishing houses are producing curricular materials which help youngsters develop new understandings about ecology, peacemaking, nuclear warfare, substance abuse, and sexuality.

An "innoculation approach" to religious education raises a number of very important questions related to the developmental match between learners and content, methodology of teaching, the relative value of traditional content compared to contemporary issues, and evaluation of the effects of such instruction upon the learners. At no level of the educational system are there less answers than for teachers of young children. Despite the growing number of commercial resources on the market for teaching preschoolers about potential abduction, sexual abuse, AIDS, and nuclear warfare through puppets, coloring books, and videotaped cartoon characters, no one knows how such information will affect their developing worldview and sense of the goodness of God's creation.

While teachers, parents, and caregivers of young children can choose whether to present this type of information, there are many harsh realities in children's lives over which they have no control. The "facts of life" for today's preschoolers are sobering indeed, as statistics from the Children's Defense Fund reveal. In America, the richest country in the world, one out of four of today's preschoolers is inadequately fed, clothed, and housed. Of the 4.3 million black children and 8.1 million white children living in poverty, 3.4 million are under the age of six. Two-thirds of all AFDC recipients are children, and nearly half of these are younger than six; their May 1987 aid payment averaged $4.04 per child per day. One out of ten has not seen a doctor during the past year, and less than half are adequately immunized; one out of six has no health insurance and would be turned away from the typical hospital emergency room. Poverty is now the greatest child killer, with more children dying from poverty each year than from traffic accidents and suicides combined.

The typical preschooler is also likely to be spending long hours each day away from his/her mother. Half of all mothers with preschool children are in the labor force; and projections are that by 1995, two-thirds of all preschoolers (some 15 million children) will have working mothers. There is a national shortage of quality, supervised childcare; and where it is available, the typical cost of full-time care in America's major cities and suburbs is $3000 for one child, about a third of the annual poverty-level income for a family of three. Only one out of five preschoolers has adequate childcare, and only 18 percent of those eligible for government programs like Head Start are provided with the services which will enhance their readiness for a successful educational experience (Children's Defense Fund, 3-13).

Many young children live stress-filled lives due to dysfunctional families. With half of all marriages ending in divorce, more than a million children, the majority of them under the age of six, must cope each year with feelings of confusion, guilt, and abandonment when adults whom they loved and trusted leave their lives. If present trends continue, 60 percent of today's toddlers will spend some part of their childhood with a single parent, most likely their mother. Infinitely more difficult for the child to understand and overcome is the family which offers abuse rather than loving care. Estimates are that some 1.5 million children each year endure physical, emotional, and sexual abuse, with their mothers being most likely to be the abuser. About 40 percent of all abused children are preschoolers; a fourth of them are infants or toddlers under the age of two who are often the result of an unplanned, unwanted pregnancy. About 1200 children die of abuse each year, and some 6000 suffer permanent brain damage from such attacks. Although abusive parents are found in all socioeconomic classes, all educational levels, and all religious backgrounds, alcohol or drug usage is a significant factor in up to 90 percent of all child abuse cases. The number of children at risk is clearly growing, since an estimated 7 million children have at least one substance-abusing parent (Brophy, et al.).

Such life experiences cause undeniable trauma to millions of young children each year. However, there are no verifiable statistics for the countless numbers of children who repeatedly experience pressure, exploitation, and devaluation in much more subtle ways as they mature in America's materialistic society. Advertisers shamelessly appeal to children's fantasies, media producers resist all efforts to consider the appropriateness of material for young viewers, and self-proclaimed "experts" peddle activities and materials guaranteed to help young parents rear a "Superbaby" (Langway, et al). Harried parents' stress-packed lives demand that young children accommodate to a pace of life which leaves little time for freedom, play, or privacy. Influenced by the national school-reform movement, schools are extending academic content and inappropriate teaching methods down into kindergarten and nursery schools, demanding that young children perform or be labeled a failure before they lose their baby teeth (Elkind, *Miseducation*). The face of childhood is rapidly changing; and as young children find themselves constantly pressured to achieve, conform, cope, and buy, the effects upon their developing personalities are only beginning to emerge.

Ken Magid, chief of psychological services at the Golden, Colorado, Medical Clinic and codirector of the Behavioral Science Department for Family Practice Physicians at St. Joseph Hospital in Denver, offers a dismal projection of the future lives of many of these children. Writing with Carole McKelvey, an award-winning journalist, Magid compellingly weaves together the findings of classic studies on infant attachment and contemporary investigations on the roots of antisocial behavior into an explanation for the rapidly rising number of persons being identified as victims of APD (Antisocial Personality Disorder). While varying in degree, the symptoms of APD are described by psychiatrists as an inability to form lasting emotional relationships; manipulative or even cruel treatment of others, ranging from desertion to physical violence; an unwillingness to follow rules and to live within society's norms and laws; and a personality characterized by total self-centeredness and the lack of a healthy conscience or feelings of remorse. Magid conservatively estimates that one out of twenty, about 13 million persons, are afflicted with some tendency toward APD, ranging along a continuum from the manipulative, "hard-sell" behaviors of the stereotypical used car salesman and shrewd politician to sadistic torture and murder by persons like Charles Manson.

As they describe the early identification and rising numbers of "Trust Bandits" among children, Magid and McKelvey cite factors under investigation as causes: "Marital discord, physical, sexual and psychological abuse or neglect; overly harsh, inconsistent discipline; genetic influences; poverty and social disadvantage; the position of the child in the family; the child's individual temperament; and child-rearing abilities" (32-3). Their thesis is that today's societal structures prevent infants and young children from accomplishing their most important developmental task, attaching to their parents. The result is that these children are mistrustful of others, filled with a deep-seated hostility, and lacking the conscience which would prevent their exploiting others. Simply put, they never learn to love. Scott Peck, a Christian psychiatrist, believes these children grow up to be evil adults. In *People of the Lie,* Peck says, "They cause suffering. The evil create for those under their dominion a miniature, sick society" (123).

Magid and McKelvey warn that solving this overwhelming societal problem will require the coordination of many psychological, government, educational, and economic resources. They advocate solutions as varied as prevention of unwanted pregnancies, especially among adolescents; education for parents about young children's emotional needs and development; upgraded training for daycare workers and teachers; improvement of child protective services in adoption, fostercare, divorce, and abuse and neglect situations; and efforts within the private economic sector to encourage pro-family policies such as extended paternal leave and sponsorship of quality childcare for employees. These recommendations are clearly in the best interests of children beset by external stressors over which they have no control, and there is a growing body of research into risk factors and resiliency in children which is encouraging in its identification of such extra-family supports that can reduce the likelihood of the child suffering life-long social and emotional impairment. In her thorough review of the research literature, Emmy Werner, Research Child Psychologist at the University of California, summarizes the findings and implications of these studies. She challenges those who care about young children struggling in a world they did not create, saying:

> Outside the family circle there are other powerful role models that give emotional support to a vulnerable child. The three most frequently encountered in studies of resilient children are: a favorite teacher, a good neighbor, or a member of the clergy. . . . The central component in the lives of the resilient children that contributed to their effective coping appeared to be a feeling of confidence or faith that things *will work out* as well as can be reasonably expected, and that the odds *can* be surmounted. The stories of resilient children teach us that such a faith can develop

and be sustained, even under adverse circumstances, if children encounter people who give meaning to their lives and a reason for commitment and caring. Each of us can impart this gift to a child—in the classroom, on the playground, in the neighborhood, in the family—*if* we care enough (72).

Helping young children acquire faith in themselves, in others, and in the ultimate goodness of life is the central task of religious educators everywhere. Researchers have documented the overwhelming numbers of "at risk" children and the likely consequences of society's failure to recognize and support those caught in circumstances which will negatively affect their developing belief and value systems. Clearly, the need is there, along with the opportunity, especially in church-sponsored childcare programs. What is far from clear, however, is exactly how faith communities should go about helping lay the foundations for personality and faith formation during the early years of a child's life.

Those charged with the religious education and nurture of young children can find many approaches, ranging from John Westerhoff's faith enculturation model to the cognitive-developmental emphasis of Ronald Goldman. Jerome Berryman, drawing upon the philosophy and pedagogy of Maria Montessori, suggests filling children's classrooms with small replicas of objects which they can manipulate in retelling and experiencing the meanings of Biblical passages. Margaret Sawin advocates teaching young children in cross-generational Family Clusters. Maria Harris emphasizes the contribution of aesthetics, Mary Wilcox, social perspective-taking, and David Elkind, play, in religious education. And, of course, there are numerous other emphases among the hundreds of denominationally-published materials for young children. Out of the dilemma of finding the "best" solution to the problems cited above, the concept of a symposium on faith development in the early childhood years was born, as a means for addressing two vitally important questions: (1) What is really known about the process by which young children form religious faith during their first years of life; and (2) given this knowledge, what should the institutional church be doing to support this process?

Through the vision and energy of Albert Gooch, President of Kanuga (Episcopal) Conferences, and William G. Baker of Los Angeles, the Ahmanson Foundation of California, Trinity Foundation of New York, and several generous individuals agreed upon the importance of such a symposium and committed themselves to underwriting it. A coordinator was chosen in early 1986, and a Steering Committee (listed in the Appendix) was recruited to begin the planning. By the time the Steering Committee met at Kanuga for a planning weekend in February 1987, it had identified the Presentors who could most effectively address those questions. Each is a rigorous scholar-researcher, respected by colleagues for the breadth and depth of his/her knowledge. In addition, all have shown the ability to think independently, to push back the frontiers of knowledge through their writings and research, and to address significant societal issues through creative applications of their ideas in church and secular settings.

Dr. James W. Fowler, Director of the Center for Faith Development at Candler School of Theology, Emory University, was invited to open and close the Symposium with addresses focusing upon the processes of personality and faith formation during the early years and the role of the church in nurturing children's nascent faith. Fowler's theory of faith development is especially useful in that it is life-span, empirically based, and integrative of those major theorists and areas of development which form the base for research-validated programs of early childhood development and education. In Fowler's view, selfhood and faith are inextricably intertwined, both beginning at birth, growing within the context of social relationships, and attaining their fullest development within a community which shares mutual trust and loyalty in triadic relationships to self, others, and God.

These addresses greatly expand Fowler's earlier descriptions of what he labels the *primal* and *intuitive-projective* stages of faith. Building upon Daniel Stern's identification of the four senses of self which emerge during the child's first two years of life, Fowler explores the beginnings of imagination, the origins of ritualization and the sense of the "numinous," the genesis of shared meanings and growth of symbolization, and the birth of the soul. Moving to the *intuitive-projective* stage, Fowler extends the work of Ana-Maria Rizzuto to explain how children construct an image of God from their interactions with parents and significant others. In Fowler's view, what happens between the child and parents or caregivers in the ordinary rituals of daily life and care profoundly affects emerging faith and selfhood. No stranger to the realities of childhood today, Fowler postulates that the existence of many weak, vulnerable, alienated persons may be due to "befallenness" created by an uncaring and unjust society rather than to the consequences of original sin. This befallenness greatly impairs the child's innate pre-potentiation for growth in selfhood and faith; and Fowler's call for "public churches" to advocate for young children is truly prophetic, a voice which must be heeded if the future of all American children is not to be imperiled.

Alice S. Honig, Professor of Child Development of Syracuse University, Research Editor of NAEYC's *Young Children*, and author of well over a hundred published research papers, was asked to speak about ways parents and caregivers might nurture the roots of faith in infants and toddlers. Like Fowler, Honig sees faith reflected in actions, and she firmly believes that children construct their faith within the context of interactions with significant adults who care for them. Her "Prescriptions for Caregivers" are grounded in the theories of Erikson, Piaget, and Mahler and in her interpretation of contemporary research ranging over many areas of child development and education. Where readers have been disquieted by the challenge of nurturing Stern's four emerging selves and Fowler's corresponding foundations of faith, they will be reassured by Honig's description of caregiver behaviors which address that need. She is most comforting in her awareness and acceptance of the needs of persons filling the parent role for the first time, and in her conviction that all parents and caregivers can be helped to understand the importance of the faith-building task and to increase their skills and satisfaction in meeting the needs of little ones during these crucial years.

Lucie W. Barber, for many years Director of Applied Research at the Character Research Project, Union College, was asked to discuss her unique approach to religious education for young children. Barber's "art-science" of attitude education utilizes persons and activities important in the child's everyday environment to lay the foundations for mature attitudes which inspire loving and responsible behavior toward others.

Barber's extensive use of learning theory in the creation of a systematic approach to teaching the "foundations of faith" may distress religious educators who believe behavioristic theory is mechanistic and its use will interfere with the developing child's free will. But Barber, who labels her approach "behavioralist," has something important to say. A careful reading of her concise, cogent explanation of this innovative approach to religious education for young children may or may not lead readers to her other writings; but it will surely help them understand why the Association of Professors and Researchers in Religious Education elected her its President in 1978.

Bettye M. Caldwell, Donaghey Professor of Education at the Center for Research on Teaching and Learning at the University of Arkansas, has long been a leader in the campaign for quality childcare programs. She was asked to focus upon the antecedents of concern for others and to recommend ways that such concern could be fostered in childcare programs, particularly those external to the home. Drawing upon the personal wisdom and professional knowledge gained in her many experiences as researcher, program administrator, government consultant, and leader of NAEYC, the nation's largest organization of early childhood professionals, Caldwell explains the important contribution church-sponsored childcare programs can make to the child's developing sense of trust in an untrustworthy world. But there is more to her presentation. As she leads her readers through a fresh look at the process by which young children learn, the content of what can be learned about oneself and others during the preschool years, and the identification of essential environmental supports for such learning, Caldwell communicates a vision of the difference it might make in this unsteady and confusing world if faith communities everywhere took seriously the possibilities of childcare as a ministry.

A major task for the Steering Committee was recruiting participants who could contribute to as well as benefit from the Symposium. As a result of its careful work in inviting and stipending well qualified persons from varied socio-economic backgrounds, institutions, and ethnic and racial groups, more than two hundred participants from thirty-three states, the District of Columbia, West Africa, and the Diocese of Hong Kong (via Boston University) attended the Symposium. Their occupations ranged from university and seminary professors and researchers to curriculum writers, diocesan/regional/national coordinators of religious education, family life ministers, and administrators of programs offering educational and childcare services to young children and their families. The Symposium was truly ecumenical in attracting persons from many faith traditions including American Baptist, Church of Christ, Disciples of Christ, Episcopal, Jewish, Lutheran (Evangelical and Missouri Synod), Mennonite, Methodist, Mormon, Presbyterian, Quaker, Roman Catholic, Southern Baptist, Unitarian, and United Church of Christ.

Such diversity was both stimulating and productive of new learnings. As a means of incorporating the rich variety of experiences, insights, and resources brought by participants, on-going Covenant Groups, "fish-bowl" reaction sessions to the Presentors' ideas, and Special Interest sessions led by Symposium members were scheduled daily. Two major needs emerged from participants during these sessions. First, many requests clustered around the need to know more about the processes of family formation and functioning: how persons come to image and commit themselves to the role of parent, the roles parents play, and the qualities displayed by parents who are effective in their roles as family leaders and faith educators. Discussions centering upon these questions resulted in the sharing of many ways that faith communities might support and advocate for families with young children. Kevin Swick, Professor of Early Childhood Education at the University of South Carolina and a frequent contributor to the field of family life education, volunteered to pull together participants' contributions into a conceptual framework for those sponsoring programs of family ministry and parent education within their faith communities. His chapter, "Strengthening Families for the Task," synthesizes countless informal mealtime conversations, scribbled newsprint sheets, and structured discussions from the "fish-bowls."

The second broad area was how Symposium participants might convey to their faith communities the importance of providing developmentally appropriate experiences of nurture and education for young children. The Reverend Robert Boone, an Episcopal parish priest, and his wife, Patricia Boone, a former Christian Education Director and now an elementary school counselor with educationally disadvantaged children, agreed to take on the task of summarizing participants' contributions and relating them to their personal parish experiences. The Boones have led many workshops on the local, state, and regional level for parents, teachers, administrators, and clergy concerned about young children's faith formation. Their chapter, "Inviting the Child into the Family of Faith," is filled with practical strategies which can be used to sensitize congregations to the faith needs of their youngest members.

Convinced of the importance of their shared goal and strengthened by the presence of a supportive community, Symposium participants struggled with the challenge of expanding their knowledge about children, faith development, and advocacy. Certainly, attendance at the Symposium did not simplify the task of religious educators. What it did was to affirm and clarify what, to some degree, they already knew: There is no one approach to the religious education of young children, and much that is presently being done needs to be re-examined. But there are six clear guidelines that emerged from the presentations and discussions of participants. In order to enhance the faith development of young children, programs of religious education and nurture must be:

1) rooted in the conviction that each stage and style of faith has its own graces and need for full expression, and no child should be "hurried" into the next stage;

2) grounded in child development and teaching/learning research;

3) personalized to the child's behavioral uniqueness and matched to his/her present developmental level;

4) geared toward helping the child develop foundational religious attitudes and behaviors rather than mastering a body of religious knowledge;

5) embedded in the child's everyday experiences and interactions;

6) focused upon enabling and supporting the child's primary caregivers in their role as faith educators.

This book has been created to share the ideas of those who attended the Kanuga Symposium on Faith Development in Early Childhood and to challenge faith communities across the nation to consider what they can and should be doing to assist young children's faith formation in a world which is all too often materialistic, overly competitive, exploitative, intolerant of anything less than perfection, and mistrustful of those who are different in any way. Hopefully, it will help those who accept the challenge to articulate and shape their own response. It offers guidance in the form of new knowledge and validation for those persons who do the incredibly important and demanding work in church-sponsored programs of nurture and education. Most important, it offers reverence for the task of faith development and for the integrity of each growing child, along with the humbling conviction that ultimately faith is a mystery, a gift from God.

Doris A. Blazer
Coordinator, Kanuga Symposium

1.

Strength for the Journey: Early Childhood Development in Selfhood and Faith

James W. Fowler

Prelude:

The Beginning of a Journey

In the quietness
In the quietness
In the dark warm-watery comfort
Sensing—ka-flum, ka-flum, ka-flum—
the heart's nearby steady beating
And the whisper of her breathing
A basic rocking rhythm.
Arpeggios of changing moods and motions
Play refrains somatic and biochemical
In harmony with vibrations

From the patterned timbre of her voice.
A seed growing silently.
In the spacious limbic pool
Embryonic acrobatics turn to
Kicking, probing restlessness
As term-time comes.
Restlessness, stilled by constriction,
Ooops into pushing sliding advance
Opening the narrow tunnel of passage.
Did ever love squeeze so hard?
Or life demand such bruising?
Head squeezed to cone-shape,
Tiny nose pressed flat,
Closed eyes squinting in the unaccustomed light
The gasping cry sputters with fluid
And the first lung-filling drags
Of on-earth-air.
Touch and handling
Towels and tenderness
Then stretched out gently
On mother's tum.
Soon, nipple with breast or bottle
And welcoming, ecstatic smiles
Celebrate

The Beginning of a Journey.

In a book called *Unfinished Man and the Imagination*, theologian Ray Hart characterizes what the discipline of fundamental theology looks into. He says, "It seeks to surprise theological meanings at their place of birth." He goes on to say, "The genesis of meaning which theology turns toward fundamentally is that in connection with the genesis of human being" (121). Our focus in this chapter is on selfhood and faith. Let's begin by defining our key terms. By selfhood I mean the evolving, subjective experience of becoming and being a person in relation. Evolving: unfolding, changing, undergoing continuing transformation. Subjective: the experience of the subject, what one experiences as he or she goes through this process of evolving, of being and becoming a person in relation. We are indelibly social selves. That deep social experience of being within the womb and then emerging to a new quality of relatedness is the only context in which we can become selves. Eventually we become reflective selves.

And then faith—another mystery. Faith also involves an evolving construction of a sense of relatedness to others and to an ultimate environment. The ultimate environment is symbolized in our culture, and in most others, by some kind of God-representation, some sort of symbol or image of an ultimate being or an ultimate reality. Faith, in addition to a sense of relatedness to ultimate being or ultimate reality, includes a sense of relatedness to the world, the neighbor, the self, in light of that ultimate relatedness. This is the pattern we call faith—a dynamic, evolving pattern for the making and the maintenance of meaning for our lives (Fowler, *Stages* 1-36).

The faith by which we live has a triadic pattern, a covenantal pattern. By "triadic" I mean that there is a relationship in which we as selves are related to others in mutual ties of trust and loyalty, of reliance and care. But that dyad is grounded in our common relatedness to centers of value and power that in some sense transcend us and are thirds in our relationship.

Figure 1.

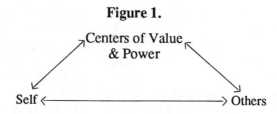

There is a triadic structure, or pattern, to our selfhood and a triadic pattern to our being in faith. Self and other, trust and loyalty, mutual trust in and loyalty to centers of meaning, value, and power—these are the dynamics of faith. In this chapter we will try to look at the origins of selfhood and faith. We have as antecedents for this work the research of others who have looked at early childhood and who have looked at faith.

The Focus on Early Childhood: Three Orienting Perspectives

The seminal work of Erik H. Erikson, on what he calls psychosocial development, has helped us look at the formation of basic trust in the first year or year and a half of life as it struggles with a sense of basic mistrust. As we emerge from that first year or so of life with, on the whole, a balance of trust over mistrust, a basic virtue of selfhood and faith emerges—a virtue which Erikson calls the strength of Hope. The philosopher Santayana refers to Erikson's Hope as "animal faith"—a kind of ground trust that one can be at home in the world, and that there is a future for this being. We begin with a ground sense of hope.

Between eighteen and thirty-six months Erikson sees the emergence of another pivotal crisis in our lives. Now able to stand on our own two feet—however wobbly—we struggle with a new sense of autonomy, of being a separate self, while maintaining enough connectedness to avoid feeling overly powerless or dominated. With sufficient autonomy we do not give in to what Erikson calls "shame and doubt" in the self. Shame and doubt in the self can constitute a pervasive sense of incapacity, inability, or inadequacy. And how vulnerable the child is to an environment that will label him or her as organismically, fundamentally inadequate—that experience of shame and doubt. Where autonomy wins a victory over shame and doubt (though it never banishes it), there emerges the virtue or the strength of personhood and faith that Erikson calls Will—the ability to assert oneself and to claim for the self what it is due. With autonomy the child learns to say "I" with conviction and to claim "my" and "mine."

Erikson next points to a period, roughly thirty-six to sixty months, which is central for a crisis he calls "initiative versus guilt." This is the capacity of the young person, now able to move and control limbs and to have purposes and ideas, to compete with others, to conspire against siblings and with siblings, to enter the playworld, the world of imagination and anticipation of future roles. At the same time s/he must come to a firm resolution or recognition that one will not be the permanent and exclusive partner of the parent of the opposite sex. This means dealing with the guilt that one feels about those contemplated desires. It means, on the whole, to evolve a sense of freedom and initiative that gives rise to the virtue of Purpose. In this stage we see the emergence of conscience, the internalization of the norms and the values that are important for the communities of which one is a part. Here we have an account of the beginning drama of the young child, according to Erik Erikson, in much abbreviated account (*Childhood and Society*).

Jean Piaget has been very helpful to us in understanding the early cognitive development of the child. He explains how a child in the first year and a half of life orders his or her view of the world largely through bodily experience of that world, in a stage or a phase he calls "sensory-motor learning." This is a pre-language way of ordering the world of objects and of persons. And then about eighteen months, give or take some time on either side, there begins to be that revolution in which language becomes important to us. Now we begin to use symbols to represent objects and persons and feelings and states. Now we enter into a stage or a phase that

Piaget characterizes as "preoperational knowing and thinking." The child's imagination runs free and ranges over his or her total experience. S/he encounters novelties each day and works to hold together in episodic constructions a grasp of the meaning-world. Feeling and perception dominate the child's ways of knowing and believing, and fantasy and makebelieve are as real to the child as what one encounters in everyday life. Piaget's drama of cognitive development gives us insights into the period that we are looking at in this chapter (*Play, Child and Reality, Psychology of Child*).

Further, I and my associates have done research in what is called faith development theory (Fowler and Keen; Fowler, *Stages of Faith;* Osmer and Fowler). Much influenced by Erikson and Piaget, we have identified two early childhood stages, the stage of *primal faith* in which the child forms that deep sense of trust and learns a rudimentary kind of relatedness to those who are close, a kind of sharing of love and of values and somatic bodily sharing of meanings. Then we find a stage that begins at about the eighteen month transition to language which we call *intuitive-projective faith.* It has many of the qualities I described for Piaget's phase of preoperational knowing.

The challenge of the Kanuga conference for me was to go behind these familiar perspectives on early childhood, with their global descriptions of this period, and to try to find more precise, more deep, and more suggestive accounts—particularly of early infancy. In that effort, let us turn to the work of a theorist of early childhood development, Daniel N. Stern. The book I want to call to your attention is Stern's *The Interpersonal World of the Infant.* Let me give some orientation to what makes Stern very special in my view. There are three features.

First of all, Stern is trained as a psychoanalyst, a psychiatrist. He has a medical background, and he stands in that tradition of psychoanalytic thinkers who try to reconstruct infant experience from the standpoint of their work with adult patients. This is an important source of knowledge of what infancy is about and what happens or needs to happen there, as well as what often doesn't happen or what can happen in wrong ways. This psychoanalytic approach tries to reconstruct infantile experience on the basis of working with adult patients. In writing his book on *Young Man Luther,* Erikson said, "At times, we will have to try to describe what would prove to have had to have been the case on the basis of clinical insight (50)." In a sense, psychoanalytic theories have reconstructed infancy on the basis of what will prove to have had to have happened for these patterns of adult personality to exist.

Second, Stern has paid careful attention and contributed to the developmental psychological study of actual infants in the process of their interaction with others and their environments. He has looked carefully at laboratory research and observational research of young children, catching them in the act of becoming persons and making meaning. What's intriguing about Daniel Stern's book is that it pulls together those two perspectives on infancy and keeps them in a kind of mutually correcting and mutually enriching tension. So with Stern, we get, from my standpoint, a kind of bifocal view of infancy that is exceedingly rich and suggestive.

In the third place, I find Stern's work very helpful for us in our interest in selfhood and faith because he gives us strong evidence of what I call "innate pre-potentiation" for selfhood and relation, on the one hand, and for faith on the other. Innate pre-potentiation—that's an important concept, though a little difficult to communicate easily. Innate means coming with the infant, genetic. Pre-potentiation means pre-ready for relatedness, pre-ready to meet an environment in the process of constructing shared meanings. It doesn't mean that this development is automatic, or that it's all genetically determined. Rather, it means that there is a readiness that depends upon the environment's readiness to meet it in a mutuality of stimulation and active responsiveness. And where that mutuality is present, the infant shows a strong predisposition to grow toward healthy relationships and to grow toward the construction of a coherent and life-sustaining sense of faith and meaning.

Emergent Selfhood and the Genesis of Faith

What does Stern offer us? He gives us a picture of four emergent senses of the self. Now let me say a word about senses of the self. Earlier I characterized selfhood as the "subjective experience of becoming a person in relation." What Stern has tried to do is to help us re-enter the infant's experience of the earliest months of life, and give us access to it as the infant experiences it. There is a great danger of our projecting back into the child on the basis of adult experience. That's part of the danger of trying to reconstruct "what will prove to have had to have been the case"—we often look at it from adult eyes and through the lenses of adult experience. Stern has tried as much as possible to get behind our memory screens and projections and to help us enter the world of the child. As we examine what Stern and his sources can teach us about the infant's experience of growth in selfhood and faith, I will ask you to refer regularly to Figure 2.

Now let us look briefly at an overview of these four emerging senses of self. Then we can go into them in more detail. Please understand that Stern believes that these emerging senses of self have separable or at least separately analyzable futures. That is to say, it's not that these different senses of self become blended into one. Rather, each of these emergent senses of self has its own future strand of integrity which will interrelate with the others. Let's look at these senses of self.

First, there's the sense of the *emergent self*, from birth to about two months. I think of this as a kind of slender trunk of a tree that will continue to grow. Here the child starts to construct from the beginning a world that's different from the self. It attends to persons as different from the self, and it responds to them in certain ways that indicate that the child is already exercising capacities to create a permanent and stable "otherness," whether the otherness is that of persons or objects. In a moment we will see that there is a particular interest in persons, even in the first two months. Next, Stern points to a sense of a *core self*. One way to understand this, I think, is to see it as a body self, the infant's experience of

Figure 2.

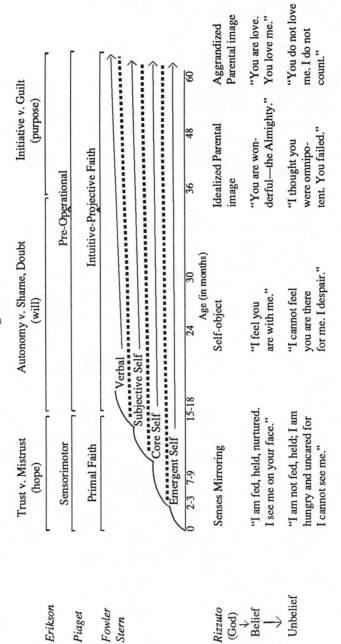

Erikson	Trust v. Mistrust (hope)		Autonomy v. Shame, Doubt (will)		Initiative v. Guilt (purpose)	
Piaget	Sensorimotor		Pre-Operational			
Fowler Stern	Primal Faith		Intuitive-Projective Faith			

Age (in months)

0 — 2-3 — 7-9 — 15-18 — 24 — 30 — 36 — 48 — 60

Emergent Self
Core Self
Subjective Self
Verbal

Rizzuto (God)	Senses Mirroring	Self-object	Idealized Parental image	Aggrandized Parental image
Belief →	"I am fed, held, nurtured. I see me on your face."	"I feel you are with me."	"You are wonderful—the Almighty".	"You are love. You love me."
Unbelief →	"I am not fed, held; I am hungry and uncared for I cannot see me."	"I cannot feel you are there for me. I despair."	"I thought you were omnipotent. You failed."	"You do not love me. I do not count."

being a body that is integral and coherent. That comes in the period of roughly two to six months.

Then there is a third sense of self that he calls the *subjective self*, or at times the *inter-subjective self*. This sense of self arises in the period of roughly seven to fifteen months. Here we have the emergence of an awareness of affect, an awareness of feeling in the self and others, and the beginning of a concern to attune the infant's affect with the affect of others. A kind of first step toward emotional intimacy emerges in that sense of self. And then, finally, there is the sense of the *verbal self*: the self that relates to others, world, and self in terms of language and symbol in more conscious ways.

Each of those senses of self has its own future. Stern, when he works with adult patients in psychiatry, listens very carefully, not just to the expressions of the verbal self but for the silences and for the themes that would indicate where repair is needed at the level of the emergent self, even for the adult. It may be that repair is needed for the inter-subjective or core self, neither of which is initially available to the verbal self. So each of these selves has its own future, and each continues to be an important part of the knowing, the selfhood, the relating, and the faith of adult persons.

The Emergent Self and the Birth of Imagination

I invite you to look with me more carefully at each of these senses of self. Let us look first at the emergent self. Perhaps you've begun to discern that the picture that Stern gives us of infancy is a somewhat different picture than Piaget, Erikson, Mahler, and others give us of the infant as a kind of undifferentiated entity in its environment. They write as though the infant is embedded in the relationship with Mother, Father, caretakers, and the objects of the world, and doesn't attend to them as separate from the self. This is Piaget's *a'dualistic* self-other relation; Stern tells us, in contrast to what we have thought for a long time, that this is not initially so. From the beginning, he contends, the baby has a rudimentary sense of separateness and otherness from that which is not the self. What evidence do we have for this?

Infants recognize, Stern finds, certain invariant properties of those persons who care for them. For example, neonates can distinguish smiling faces from surprised faces. Researchers have observed the infant habituate to the smiling face and then be intrigued by the contrast of the surprised face. We see that they are conserving in memory the features that constitute those expressions on faces. The young baby, prior to two months, evaluates the social world in terms of its conformity to or its discrepancy from previous patterns of experience. So from the beginning, it seems, we are constructing some sense of what is regular and what is to be depended on in the environment, and we note that which surprises us or which deviates from our expectations.

Furthermore, there is good evidence that the human form is more than a perceptual array in a kind of neutral sense and that it is very early preferred by the child. By one month, infants prefer live faces to geometric ones. They seem to respond globally to animation, to complexity, and to the configurations of faces rather than to specific facial features. A smile alone won't elicit very much just drawn on a geometric or a flat surface. There seems to be an innate preference for the topography of faces. Further, infants under two months discriminate by smell their mothers' milk from the milk of other mothers. They discriminate their own mothers' voices from others, and they seem innately predisposed to select their mothers from all others.

Recently a person who works with very young infants told me about an extremely premature baby that had to be supported for a long period by an incubator. This meant long separations from the mother. But it happened that one of the physicians, a woman who worked with this child, had a voice whose timbre and sound was very similar to the mother's. The medical staff noticed that when this particular physician was on shift, the baby's need for oxygen and other life support diminished markedly; the baby pinkened just at the sound of this particular doctor's voice. Then when this doctor left the shift, the baby sunk down again and had to be supported by the machinery. In this very first period of our lives we are forming rudimentary patterns of attachment, and we seem to exert innate preferences for the human face and for *particular* human others.

Infant behavior provides, says Stern, further evidence for this construction of a coherent otherness. Infant experience involves amodal and cross-modal knowing. What do we mean by amodal and cross-modal knowing? Amodal perception refers to a kind of perceptual unity in which we use different senses, but seem automatically to translate the perceptions gained through one sense into correlation with the perceptions gained in another sense. How do we learn to do that? It seems to be innately given, an extraordinary gift. As we look into this remarkable capacity we come close to the genesis of imagination. If faith involves the composing of a coherent and meaningful world, and a sense of relatedness to a transcendent other, then imagination is an important, even foundational part of faith. In this very earliest period of infancy, we are seeing the rudimentary manifestations of imagination—the capacity to link sensory input from one modality with that of another, so as to form an understanding that's not given in perception. This is the beginning of imagination.

How do we know that children do this amodal and cross-modal knowing? Stern draws on brilliant experimentations at this point. In one experiment, blindfolded infants are given one or another of two nipples, either a smooth nipple or a gnurled nipple. They suck the nipple, then the nipples are displayed before them. Infants will visually prefer the particular nipple that they were sucking. Now how does a baby know this? It's the transposition of the *felt* sense of the nipple to the *visual* sense of the nipple.

In a second experiment we learn that at six weeks babies notice discrepancies between speech and lip movements. We've all seen television film reruns where the voice is just a little behind the movement of the mouth. That impression is very disturbing to an infant of six weeks. They expect correlation between sound and the visual sight of lip movement.

In the third place, research demonstrates that infants experience, even in these first two months, vitality affects. What are vitality affects? They are the surges, the fadings, and the plateaus of feeling that are elicited by the vital processes of hunger and sleep and care. The infant experiences and responds to these vitality affects within, and to the vitality affects demonstrated externally by parents or other caretakers. By employing the amodal perception that we have been exploring, the infant experiences the stroking of the mother trying to calm the child and saying, "There, there, there," as a kind of diminishing vitality affect that brings comfort and assurance. We are seeing here the birth of imagination—the capacity to relate to a world of otherness and to begin to construct and link understandings and feelings about that world through the amodal and cross-modal constructions with which infants seem to be gifted.

The Core (Body) Self and the Birth of Ritualization

Now let us attend to a second level of selfhood, the emergence of the core self, the body self. I link this, in terms of its contribution to faith, to the birth of ritualization, to the birth of the body's participation in the construction of meanings. Between the second month and somewhere around six to eight months, the infant acquires a sense of self as distinct from others, though at this period he or she does not have the self as an object of reflection. This is not a reflective awareness of self. Rather, it is an experience of separateness from the other, and of the otherness of the other. The baby experiences being an integrated body, able to control its own actions, owning feelings, and sensing the continuity of the self and others.

Stern points to four basic experiences of the self, all of which are dependent upon bodily interaction and the forming of this sense of the core self. (a) There is the experience of self-agency. The baby can regularly reach for and bang a rattle and can meaningfully repeat that activity. S/he has a sense of the control of the body in being able to do that. This provides for (b) the experience of self-coherence, that one is a unified body with a kind of integrity. Whether mobile or still, the baby has a sense of being a non-fragmented, physical whole, with external boundaries and a continuous location of action. (c) The baby begins to sense self-affectivity, self-feeling. S/he becomes accustomed to patterns of feeling and emotion which are tied to the experience of self. Then (d) in a very rudimentary but important way, the baby begins to have a sense of temporal continuity, the expectation that things will repeat, that there is an order to things, and that there is a future to come. All of these are indications of the formation of self over against, or in differentiation from, others. This constitutes the first level in the emergence of the core self. It comes at age six or seven months.

With regard to the second level of the core self, we are talking about the first experience of the self in its relationship with others. Stern helps us to reflect on the fact that from two to six months, the experience of the baby—apart from when it's sleeping—is almost exclusively social. Perhaps the absence of mobility, the inability to move on one's own, lends power to the social presence of others as being of primary importance to the baby of this age. In its orientation to sociality, the baby seems to prefer higher-pitched voices and close proximity of communication, which succeeds in recruiting the parents to participate in baby talk and face-making.

This second level of core self relatedness gives rise to two very interesting concepts that Stern imputes to the infant's experience. First we learn of the phenomenon Stern calls Representations of Interactions that have been Generalized (RIGs). Earlier I likened the core self's emergence to beginnings of ritualization. Here we see the infant convert regular social interactions into generalized patterns of familiarity and expectation. The baby expects that they will be repeated and learns how to participate in them. We are seeing the beginnings of ritualization.

The essential structure of the game "peek-a-boo" is one of the RIGs that we form early in infancy. The great excitement about peek-a-boo becomes how to expand that structure to innovative extensions of its basic pattern. There are so many different ways we can modify that kind of ritual action. But further, this is evidence that the infant is constructing RIGs that capture repeated patterns of action experienced with the parents and others with whom he or she regularly interacts. We can call these constructions working models of the parental figures, or significant others. These working models are dynamic. They continue to evolve and change as the infant has new experiences and as s/he offers new initiatives in relation to the parents.

The construction of working models of others leads to the construction of what Stern calls "evoked companions." The RIG that is an evoked companion refers to a sense of the self with others, even when the others are absent. This is the capacity to feel the reassuring sense of the presence of the other with the self, even when the other is absent. The evoked companion is a sense of the invisible presence of a self-other which can make one feel comfortably affirmed in his or her total self. The relationship is embedded in specific episodes or interactional rituals which become generalized even before object permanence is intact. Even before the seven or eight month time when Piaget tells us object permanence is fully acquired, there is the possibility, it seems, of constructing this evoked companion. This construction is not yet a true transitional object because that requires more conscious symbolic activity than is possible here. But it is the construction of a reassuring presence.

Ken Brockenbrough, in conversations about these matters, has suggested that that which we call the numinous, the sense of the presence of a divine, transcendent, and reassuring reality, is related to and has its origins in the experience of the evoked companion. This seems to tie in with Erik Erikson's suggestion that in feeding, we have prolonged periods in which the infant's face and eyes encounter the mirroring presence of the animated eyes and face of the mother, father, or their substitute. This same presence, with its confirming regard, may be evoked as an antidote to anxiety when the child is alone, or as an exuberant observer when the child is actively interacting with its environment.

The Subjective Self and the Birth of the Soul

This brings us to a third level of emergent selfhood: the sense of the subjective self. Here we are present at what we may call the "birth of the soul." Parenthetically, the concept of soul has fallen on hard times, at least in Protestant Christian culture. We don't use the term much any more unless we're talking about the "eternal salvation of the soul." As important as that is, I'd like to reclaim an older sense of the soul as the seat of emotion, intuition, and receptivity to God, and to others, deep within us (Hillman). If we take that older understanding of soul seriously, we see that the emergence of the subjective self is properly called the birth of the soul.

Let us look at the subjective self. Here we see the emergence in interpersonal relations of shared frameworks and fantasies. Around seven to nine months there is the beginning of the first deliberate sharing of psychic space. Let me remind you that the Greek for soul is "psyche." Psychic states, soul states. Now how do we infer that there is a kind of inter-subjectivity taking form here? We recognize mutual constructing and sharing of feelings because we observe infants and mothers, infants and others, confirming interintentionality, demonstrating a shared attention to a third object or a third experience. We also infer this awakening of soul intimacy through the child and mother's use of pre-language expressions of shared intent. And then we see patent evidences of shared affect, communicated both from the child to the parent, from the parent back to the child, shared in clearly celebrative ways.

Let me try to make these matters clearer. To recognize and to share attention, intention, and feelings requires some shared framework of meaning, and some means of communication such as gestures, postures, and facial expressions. Here we are present at the birth of the construction of shared meanings. At this juncture in the infant's life, psychic intimacy becomes a real possibility. At the same time, the infant begins to determine the extent of self-disclosure that s/he seeks. The infant begins to have some control regarding how much of the feelings s/he is having will be expressed or shared. Again, this is not a conscious reflection and choice. It is more a kind of organismic and psychic response and initiative that the child has in an unreflective way. What's the evidence to support Stern's claims? First, we see evidence that infants do enter into experiences of shared attention with their caregivers. Nine month olds both point and can follow the imaginary line extending from the pointing finger of the mother or others. Even earlier infants are found to follow the mother's line of vision when she turns her head. More important nine-month-olds will look back to the mother to confirm the accuracy of their own gaze. There is then a triangulation, a triadic pattern, between two people and an object of their mutual interest and reference.

Second, there is shared intention. Prior to language, infants will persistently signal, through some familiar posture or gesture, that an intent is meant to be understood by another. The most basic form of this is the child's reaching to and pointing toward an object and saying "Uh! Uh! Uh!" This may be the true beginning of language. Babies also give the signal for the beginning of familiar games, such as "Horsie" or "Pat-a-cake." One year olds have repeatedly been noted to share some event with an older sibling by laughing, for reasons often unavailable to the adult observers of this mirthful scene. There can be a kind of teasing present here that adults often miss, suggesting shared mental and affective states among the siblings.

And then there's the important matter of shared affect, shared feelings. When a twelve month old faces an uncertain situation, such as a novel toy, a wall socket, or a steep set of declining stairs, he or she will likely reference to the facial expression of the parent or the caretaker in order to determine how to proceed. If the caretaker's face communicates anxiety, the baby's will also, and s/he will turn away from the new situation. This is true in completely novel situations, and it seems not to be merely an associational task. Studies that Stern reports suggest that by nine months, infants are aware of the congruence or the fit of a facial expression of another with their own affective state. In one experiment, after a troubling separation from their mothers, children preferred to look at a sad face rather than a happy face. This occurs before many infants are aware of their own facial expressions in a mirror. This evidence signals a visual proprioceptive match which is part of the amodal perspective-taking of the infant. Stern tells us that affective exchange is the most powerful and the most pervasive of the three shared states during this period of the emergence of the inter-subjective self.

Now we must take another step in this phase of the subjective self as we follow Stern. This is the important phenomenon that he calls "affect attunement." Stern's most important contribution to our study of faith and selfhood is probably his description of affect attunement as a restatement by the parent of the child's affective state. This is a complex operation and requires several important factors. First, there must be an accurate reading of the baby's behavior by the parent or other caretaker. Second, this requires an intimate history with the child's feelings, giving rise to the ability to participate in those feelings. Third, it requires the ability to respond with different, non-imitative, but accurate behaviors which signal to the infant that its affective states are understood. This means a kind of response in a different mode that says, "I'm reading you and I'm responding in rhythm, in pattern, in synchronicity with your feelings." And finally, the infant must be able to read that response for emotional attunement to occur. This complex phenomenon is very close to mirroring in the psychoanalytic sense of Kohut and others, but it is different. In Stern's interpretation, the affective state is already fully present in the infant and is not created by the mirroring presence of the parent. So we get an authentic initiative of affect from the infant to the parent which is then responded to in the creation of a mutuality or sharing.

It's important to note that attunement of this sort falls short of true empathy. It is not consciously mediated by cognitive processes which abstract the state from the person. However, think how important, in a continuing way in our lives, this kind of affect attunement is, even between persons who are capable of verbal communication. And consider how sometimes our affect attunement gives us insights that our verbal communication obscures or distorts.

I find it fascinating to look at some of the instances that Stern and others have studied in order to understand the ways infants interact with their primary caretakers as regards this business of attunement. Let me give you two examples of these. One of the prime ways that we indicate to a child that we are resonating with them or feeling with them is through matching the intensity of our responses to the intensity of their actions. An example would be when the loudness of a mother's vocal response matches the force of an abrupt arm movement that an infant makes. Let me quote Stern's account here:

> A ten-month-old girl finally gets a piece in a jigsaw puzzle. She looks toward her mother, throws her head up in the air, and with a forceful arm flap, raises herself partly off the ground in a flurry of exuberance. And the Mother says, "Yes! Thata girl!" (141).

The "Yes!" is intoned with much stress, it has an explosive rise that echoes the girl's fling of gesture and posture. It says, "I see you! I rejoice with you! I share that exuberance!" Or, take the case of "temporal beat." A regular pulsation in time is matched by the response of the parenting one:

> A 9-month-old boy bangs his hand on a soft toy, at first in some anger, but gradually with pleasure, exuberance, and humor, he sets up a steady rhythm. Mother falls into the rhythm and says, "Ka-bam! Ka-bam! Ka-bam!" with the "bam" falling on the stroke and the "Ka" riding with the preparatory upswing and the suspenseful holding of the arm before he allows it to fall (140).

These samples indicate the kind of amodal, cross-modal responses that signal attunement and build a kind of mutuality of affect between caring ones and the infants. Attunement is a dynamic, ongoing process rather than a discrete set of episodes or categorical affect. Notice that in these ritualizations of behavior, we are seeing the emergence of pre-verbal, pre-symbolic, and yet proto-symbolic activity. We are seeing communication at work here, through the use of analog and through the use of symbolic motions and movements. We are seeing the ritualization of a more conscious and collaborative sort between caretaker and infant.

One of the most fascinating things to me is the following paragraph from Stern, who talks about an important dimension of this affect attunement that seems to me to have particular reference for faith—and for selfhood, for that matter:

> Many thinkers in France and Switzerland have independently approached the problem of affect attunement along similar lines to those that we have spoken about here, and they have pushed the notion of maternal interpretation into richer clinical territory. They assert that mother's meanings reflect not only what she observes, but also her fantasies about who the infant is and who he or she is to become. Inter-subjectivity for them ultimately involves inter-fantasy. They have asked how the fantasies of the parent come to influence the infant's behavior and ultimately to shape the infant's own fantasies. This reciprocal fantasy interaction is a form of created interpersonal meaning at the covert level. Such meanings have been called "interactions fantasmatique" (134).

At Advent for Christians there is an attending to a birth, and a mothering, and the beginning of a life of very special quality. This business of the fantasies of the mother being available for the infant's attunement to them puts special significance on the eighteenth and nineteenth verses of Luke 2, where it says, after the visit of the shepherds to the newborn and the mother, "And all who heard it wondered at the things which they were told by the shepherds, but Mary treasured up all these things, pondering them in her heart." Harry Denmon said, in a kind of liberating irreverence, "Who would Jesus have been, without Mary to teach him to love, and Joseph to teach him to work, and John the Baptist to tell him who he was?"

Please note here that the triadic structure of faith emerges with this inter-subjective phase of selfhood. There is an attending to third realities between the parent and child, including shared fantasies as a third reality between them. And there is the sharing of meanings prior to language that relate to those thirds. This is the triadic structure of faith mentioned at the beginning of this chapter. It is interesting to speculate on the contribution of the evoked companion that we mentioned earlier—the reassuring sense of presence emergent at the core self level to this more complex business of affect attunement and symbolization.

The Verbal Self and the Birth of Symbolization

We come now to the fourth sense of self, the verbal self. Here I want to speak about the contribution to faith of the birth of symbolization. At age fifteen months, our oldest daughter Joan still—despite Freudian warnings to the contrary—lived in the bedroom of her mother and father, in a graduate student apartment where there wasn't another bedroom. She would wake up in the morning at about six o'clock—an annoying time for people who had studied late in the night—and reconstitute the world by naming it. She would stand in her crib and point at the light and say "Yite?" and insist that there be a chorus from the sleepy Greeks in the bed—"Yes, that's a light..." She would name the fifteen or eighteen objects in that room that she knew the names of. Then with this ritual completed, it was as though the day could now begin. The world had been reconstituted; it had been named; everything was in its place. There had been this ritual of confirmation and now we could get on with the day. What we were seeing here, I think, was the exuberant discovery that things do have names and that we can refer to them in ways other than pointing or grasping. Persons have names, and we can talk about things that aren't present to us, even talking about feelings and thoughts. What an exhilarating new step in life language and the conscious use of symbolization bring!

Note in Figure II that the emergence of the verbal self corresponds with a watershed time in each of the theories that we're relying upon. Erikson sees it as decisive in the transition from basic trust to autonomy versus shame and doubt. Piaget sees it as the hallmark of the transition from sensory-motor knowing to preoperational knowing. In faith development theory we see it as the threshold of transition from primal to intuitive-projective faith; and although I don't have Margaret Mahler's work there, the time of this transition is co-terminus with the beginning of what Mahler calls "rapprochment," the second stage of differentiation, giving rise to a second birth, or the psychological birth of the infant (Mahler, Pines and Bergman).

Let's think for a few moments about language, symbol, image, and representation. The rise and use of verbal symbols is exhilarating, liberating, and yet it's full of potential for alienation as well as for communication. Consider the power of language. We are now no longer limited to pointing or gesturing with the face or hands. It is now no longer necessary to limit communication to objects that are present and concrete. We may refer to objects or persons who are away from us. We may begin to refer to feelings and to more intangible dimensions of our experience. We may begin to name and represent qualities of persons and relations. Of course all this begins in a rudimentary way, quite concretely. But the capacities that we have seen emerging with each of the phases of selfhood have underscored the importance of feelings in communication. They have also pointed to the natural precursors of symbolic communication and representation. We saw anticipations of this in the amodal and the synthesial capacities of the pre-linguistic child's shaping of experience. We saw it in the capacity to construct and be comforted by evoked companions. We saw it in the abilities to generalize from events and to shape working models for persons and rituals. And we saw it in the capacities for affect attunement. All of these qualities bespeak the forming of abilities to employ sign and symbol, metaphor and analog, narrative and meter.

Let us think about the tacit and explicit in our communication with each other. Language and symbolization create wonderful new possibilities. They bring the ability to communicate about objects, persons, feelings, and shared understandings. They make possible the objectification of our experienced world. They give us the capacity to stop our world and to interrogate it as an object of our experience. We gradually become able to hold dimensions of our experience up for our examination or for joint consideration with others. But our naming and symbolization of experiences are never fully adequate or fully complete. Always, in our efforts at communicating our experiences, our knowledge, or our feelings, we must deal with a broad gap between what we see and feel, on the one hand, and what we can say, on the other.

Michael Polanyi states this succinctly: "We know more than we can tell" (4). He reminds us that much of our knowing and doing remain inaccessible to both our consciousness and our ability to communicate. He calls these crucial dimensions of our knowing the tacit dimension. Because our sense of self has profound and continuing dimensions that are pre-verbal at the levels of the core self and the subjective self, there are aspects of our selves and our meanings that are capable of verbal expression only at the cost of significant distortion and reduction. From eighteen months on through early childhood we make remarkable progress at utilizing language and symbols to communicate with others. Nonetheless, in this early period, it remains a beginning process. We work a lifetime to bring our most significant knowing and experiencing to expression. Words and symbols are increasingly helpful to us, but there is always the danger—even the inevitability—that our verbal and symbolic expressions of self and our meanings will distort, reduce, and neglect.

Language and Selfhood: The Danger of the False Self

The subjective self, which Stern has described prior to the advent of language, is experienced by the infant as separate from others. That sense of selfhood, however, is not yet an object for self-recognition. With the advent of symbol and language, the infant has at his or her disposal the tools to objectify, to distort, and to transcend experiences of the self and the world at large. What is this prelinguistic child's experience of alienation or distortion in the first year and a half? Stern makes vague references to "narcissistic injuries" experienced within the primary relationships, which he calls "primitive agonies." These are unnamed agonies, agonies before we have the language to give voice to them, or the objective capacity to reflect and say, "I'm hurting." Primitive agonies which we suffer without words, without ways of reflectively communicating about them. In some sense we simply are our agonies at this stage. Stern believes, however, that neurotic experiences of anxiety and the forming of distorting defense mechanisms come after the experience of the self as objective through the use of language. Stern recognizes that a child may experience discontinuity and actual disruption in core and inter-subjective relatedness, but he insists that anxiety as "the fear of ceasing to be" or of ceasing to be loved entails positioning oneself via representation and objectification as an object in the immediate future. Therefore, he suggests, true anxiety experiences are a post-linguistic matter. Real anxiety comes after we've acquired a sense of the verbal self.

Insofar as I understand Stern's position here, I think I differ with him. It seems to me that each level of emergent selfhood represents a place at which mutuality, worth, shared meanings, and organismic well-being are at stake and at risk. We are vulnerable at each of these levels. While the child's self-aware appropriation of these experiences will not take form until after the advent of language, failures or violations of mutuality at any and each of these levels can have profound effects on the forming self. Moreover, the readiness for what Mahler calls "rapprochment"—the second, more self-aware experience of separation—seems to me to depend upon strengths of prelinguistic selfhood built in the mutuality and the rebalancing of self-other relationships in each of the prior phases of emergent selfhood (Mahler, Pines and Bergman).

What is clear, in any case, is that with the advent of language, vast new potentials for alienation and for the inculcation of shame and doubt emerge. About eighteen months a child who has surreptitiously had a red spot of rouge placed on the nose will, upon seeing the self reflected in a mirror, point to the rouged spot on its own face. The child shortly afterwards will use "I," "me," and "mine" in appropriate ways. Children at this age also will begin to manipulate replicas of family members—sets of dolls which they will match with family members—and take an interest in family pictures. There is a beginning capacity to objectify the self as a body self, and to hold in memory representations of self and significant others. For the first time in its young life, the child is in a position to negotiate with the parent to determine how transparent or isolated he or she will become psychically in the quest for mutuality. A child now has the beginnings of reflective choice about what s/he will disclose and what will not be disclosed—what is safe to disclose and what is not safe to disclose.

At this juncture, however, the maintenance of one's integrity in the face of inner and outer experiences of threat can be sought through dangerous defense mechanisms such as repression, disavowal, and denial. In each case where these dangerous defense mechanisms emerge, a path between experience and feeling, between feeling and language, and between language and experience, is broken. Defenses break the linkages between experience and feeling and language. And we begin, consciously or unconsciously, to deceive others and to deceive ourselves.

This description gives rise to the construction of what has been called a "false self" (Winnicott). By this we mean a representation of self to self and others which makes existence possible and bearable in the midst of severely depriving, distorting, or constricting relational circumstances. The false self can be constituted in a necessary over-identification with the self's conforming to exceedingly harsh prohibitions or taboos. It can adapt the twisted posture required in a family situation which places mutually contradictory demands upon the child—the classic doublebind is a strategy of survival in a deeply threatened relational matrix. It severs the child's relation and reliance upon its own preverbal experiences. Its defense strategies require the child's collusion—against the true self—with the structure of denials and lies of the crippled family's ways of relating to each other. It gives rise to unreality and severe discontinuity between the past experiences of the subjective self and the present experience of the objective self. If these patterns of defense persist, there is every likelihood that the false self will become ascendant. This may protect the inadequacies of the true, preverbal self, but it will be sundered, cut off from below, which is the immanence of one's becoming, from those primal experiences of the earlier phases of selfhood which could fund and support further growth. And it will be cut off from above, from the consolidation toward a mutual future from the formation of what Mahler calls "constancy," the internalization of a firm sense of the true self and the reliable presence of others within the self.

Language, Ritualization and Meaning

Symbol and story, healthy adaptation and attachment, make manifest the fruits of constancy and consolidation. With the emergence of the verbal self, meaning is now mediated by language and symbol. Meaning is created between parents and others and the child in new levels of mutuality. This is Martin Buber's notion of the meaning that mediates and arises between us in our relationships, the essence of symbolic and verbal mutuality. Just as language is a tool for distancing and separation, it is also a tool for communion. Words represent the medium through which different minds and experience-worlds can be united in episodes of shared meaning.

Katherine Nelson, Jerome Bruner, and their colleagues describe an episode where, upon the birth of a younger brother, the two year old sister devises all sorts of ways to keep the father present with her at bedtime. At his eventual departure, she adopts his tone and mannerisms in an ongoing monologue. Besides practicing language, she is objectively demonstrating her internalization of her father's total presence. If successful, the child gains agency; she keeps Dad present. She gains autonomy, being able to relinquish his physical presence. She gains communion, because she now participates in his symbol system and mannerisms, all by way of this simple bedtime ritual (qtd. in Stern, 172-73). This, then, is the opposite of alienation; it keeps her from having to construct a false self. The emanating power of becoming, coming up from below, meets with the transcendent or the numinous power of the future in language and ritual, and a relatively true self is consolidated in an early interpersonal dance.

Following Erik Erikson for a bit, let us consider what each stage of early childhood contributes by way of ritualization and the sharing of meanings. More than any other social scientist, Erikson has suggestively indicated the contribution that each developmental life stage makes to our total capacity as adults, to be ritualizers and celebrators of shared meanings (*Toys*). What does Erikson tell us about infancy? In earliest infancy, we come to our first awareness, in the presence and under the care of powerful ones upon whom we are dependent. We come to such an awareness in the midst of everyday rituals, of feeling and tending and cleansing and putting to bed and getting up. But in these everyday rituals we also take on the identity that is provided by the names we are given. In mutuality of recognition, in which we are called by name and given a name to call the one or the ones upon whom we are dependent, we have the primordial experience of that which Erikson calls the numinous, the mysterious, the transcendent. The sense of an evoked companion that is transcendent.

Religious traditions and the institutions of religion have evolved in societies to take principal care of the rituals that relate us to the numinous. Writing about the reenactment and ritual of our earliest experiences of knowing the Other, Erikson says, "The believer, by appropriate gestures, confesses his or her dependence and childlike faith and seeks by appropriate offerings to secure the privilege of being lifted up to the very bosom of the divine, which indeed may be seen to graciously respond with the faint smile of an inclined face" (*Toys*, 89-90).

Erikson says that one of the primordial and recurring deep religious nostalgias of the human being is the longing for the face that blesses and the eyes that recognize. And that when we return to the Eucharist and times of worship, part of what we deeply hunger for is that recognition by the transcendent and that blessing that comes. Identifying a fundamental and continuing element in all identity and ritualization, all selfhood and ritualization, Erikson says, "The numinous assures us of separateness transcended and yet also a distinctiveness confirmed" (*Toys*, 90). A separateness transcended—we really do belong to something cosmic and ultimate. And a distinctiveness confirmed—we really are separate creatures who have their own dignity and worth. And both of those are held together. This is the very basis of a sense of "I" which is renewed by the mutual recognition of all "I's" joined in a shared faith in one all-embracing "I am."

If infancy offers our first experience of the mutuality of ritualization and of the numinous, the next stage of toddlerhood and first autonomy sees the emergence of a sense of law and lawfulness which Erikson associates with the judicious. This judicious dimension becomes an element in all ritualization, for, as Erikson points out, there is no ritual up to the last judgment itself which does not imply a severe discrimination between the sanctioned, the permitted, and the out-of-bounds. In this stage (toddlerhood), the child begins to form the awareness of taboo, the forbidden, the prohibited, and with it, the inner sense of danger that one might become the very kind of person against whom all prohibitions, taboos, and boundaries are established. The birth of negative selfhood, the potential of negative identity. Theologically, we are in touch here with the emerging sense of sins, in the plural. Breaches of the forbidden. We're also in touch with sinfulness, a pervasive shame at being the rebellious one who was made curious and lured into violations by the presence of the walled-off and the prohibited. At stake in the ritualizations of this stage is the experience of a judicious authority who has set limits and judges in accordance with them, but who does so on the basis of love, protection, and out of the desire for righteousness, for right-relatedness in relationships.

Now also in the intuitive-projective stage, we include the period of the play age. Here the fantasy and pretend of children enables them to rehearse dramas of heroic and significant possible futures. Says Erikson, "Childhood play, in experimenting with self and self images, as well as images of otherness, is most representative of what psychoanalysis calls the 'ego ideal'." What is the ego ideal? Erikson calls it:

> ...that part of ourselves we can look up to. At least so far as we can imagine ourselves as ideal actors in an ideal plot. With the appropriate punishment and exclusion of those who do not make the grade. Thus we experiment with and, in a visionary sense, get ready for a hierarchy of ideal and evil roles which of course go beyond that which daily life could permit us to engage in (*Toys*, 101).

The dramatic and the playful capacities of this stage make us, potentially at least, creative and ready participants at any age in the dramas of sacrament and liturgy. Coupled with the high dignity of the judicious and the transcendent realties of the numinous, the dramatic enables us to join with others in corporate enactments and celebrations of the actuality, the presence, and the power of God.

Early Childhood and Construction of the God-Representation

I turn now to the work of Ana-Maria Rizzuto, whose book, *The Birth of the Living God,* I commend to your interest and attention. Dr. Rizzuto is both a devout Roman Catholic and a devout Freudian psychoanalyst. She's a rigorous scholar and a wonderful human being. I would like to tell you just a bit about her work in studying the emergence of God-representations in early childhood. For purposes of following this discussion, you may want to attend to Figure II. For a moment, however, let me orient you to the principal theses of *The Birth of the Living God.*

The first thesis is that there is no child in our society, who does not, by the age of about six years, construct some representation of God. Please understand that it's possible for us to have a representation of God in which we do not believe, or to which we are not attached, or which we do not find sustaining, or which we do not find positive. We are not saying that a child has a positive and a believable image in the sense of having his or her heart attached to that representation. But every child, says Rizzuto, constructs such a representation. In our own research we've found this to be true.

One of the most interesting cases where this was vindicated came when we interviewed the six year old daughter of a man and a woman who both happened to be children of clergy. So negative had been this couple's early experiences of faith and church that they resolved that they would try to deprive their own child of any exposure to religious language. They were going to try to raise a "healthy" child. When we interviewed their daughter, we found that their efforts had not succeeded. She had constructed a very interesting, if somewhat primitive, representation of God. When we probed to find the sources, we found two primary ones. One was the television show then being presented called *Bonanza.* If you remember that Western, with its story of life on the ranch with Little Joe and Hoss and Papa Cartwright, occasionally there were weddings or funerals depicted which made a big impression on this religion-starved child. She was intrigued with questions about the hymns and to whom the prayers were offered. Far more satisfying and informative to her was the Lutheran Church in America's television series, *Davy and Goliath,* the animated cartoon series in which Davy and his dog had adventures from week to week. There she saw stories that portrayed the love and care Davy gave to friends and strangers and located the source of that care in God. In her forbidden fascination, this child lived up to Rizzuto's claim that in our society every child creates some representation of God from a variety of sources.

Second, Rizzuto refutes Sigmund Freud's claim that the God-representation comes from the boy's resolution of the Oedipal struggle and castration anxiety through the projection of a benign but stern father image onto the universe. She agrees that the projection dynamic is an important one, but she rejects Freud's version of it for two reasons. First, it gives no account of how and why girls construct God-representations, so it has to be incomplete. Second, and more seriously, she claims the God-representation begins before the Oedipal period, before four or five, and has its origin earlier in the infant's life. And, most important, she suggests that the God-representations in her research draw from both the parental *imagoes,* both Mama and Papa, and perhaps other significant adults who are present in the life of the child.

The third thesis Rizzuto offers: The representation of God takes form in the space between parents and the child. This is the same space in which D. W. Winnicott says we construct transitional objects. This British object-relations language is a very mechanistic language for talking about human beings; and when we are talking about transitional objects, we're talking about symbolic representations of our relatedness to important other persons. The Linus blanket that the toddler drags around is a transitional object, symbolizing the security, the care, and the assurance of return of the beloved and trustworthy parents. Or the teddy bear is a transitional object that symbolizes the qualities of steadfastness and love. Now God takes form in that same space, says Rizzuto, and becomes a transcending representative of what Mahler called constancy.

What kind of transitional object is God? Says Rizzuto in her fourth thesis, God is a very particular and unique kind of transitional object. Children construct many others—images of monsters, representations of the devil, representations of superheroes—all of those are transitional objects that capture the child's imagination at certain periods in their childhood. But God is different from all of those, different from the Linus blankets and the teddy bears, because with God there is no object there on which the symbolization can be projected. Of course there are pictures of Jesus; and when we interview four, five, and six year olds and ask them about God, occasionally one will go and get a picture of Jesus and bring it back to us. The transitional object does have a face for that child. But for many others it doesn't have a face, as in the four year old who, when we asked about God, said that "God is everywhere, God is like the air." He had no physical representation for God.

There is no tangible model on which God can be based. The other significant difference between God and the other transitional objects we mentioned—the devil, monsters, superheroes, witches and so forth—is that there is an adult world which takes God very seriously. There are cathedrals, art, and architecture, solemn ceremonies, and impressive people using their most adult voices, addressing this Other. There are powerful "actualizations" of the reality of God inviting children to construct their mental representations of God.

At about thirty months, says Rizzuto, about the time that the consolidation and separation that Mahler calls constancy emerges, and about the time language begins to flourish as a medium for examining the environment, children make the discovery that human beings create and cause things to be. Here begins that line of questions that we are all familiar with. "What is this? How did this come to be? Who made it? Why? Where did it come from? What's it for?" That infinite regress of how things came to be leads back to the point where the parent either loses patience or cannot say where this came from, and so we say, "God made it, God is the Creator." And the child begins to learn that no one created God. Like Aristotle, the child constructs her/his own notion of the Unmoved Mover, *the primum mobile*.

How does the child construct this transitional object that we call God? Rizzuto's thesis is that when the child looks for analogs of an almighty, mysterious, transcendent, loving, caring Other, the child looks to those experiences he or she has had of those qualities, and looks to one or the other or both of the parental *imagoes*. The construction, the representation of God, draws upon the child's experiences with the parents or their surrogates and has some of the characteristics of the parental figure or figures.

The God-representations children form based on their parental models have both some of the strengths and virtues and some of the flaws and blind spots of the parental *imagoes*. Rizzuto suggests that children do idealize their representations of God so as to correct for and compensate for some of the deficiencies of the actual parents. In fact, God-representations can do a great deal to replace, restore, and heal the wounds from absent or badly distorting parents. In our round of interviews about ten years ago, repeatedly we found a certain group of persons who had lost one parent or the other before the age of five. We found that often these persons had constructed a representation of God to which they had attached with immense power. So deepgoing and primal was their attachment to God that we called them "totalizers," persons whose relationship to God was so integral to their selfhood that they could more easily imagine the loss of the self than they could imagine loss of God. The conception of a faith that contained doubt had very little meaning for these persons because their God-representation had played such a significant part in their finding and maintaining a sense of security after the death of a parent.

Examine now the lower part of Figure II for a brief look at Rizzuto's account of the relationship between the construction of a God-representation and the possibilities of belief and unbelief from her psychoanalytic standpoint. You see that in the very first stages of infancy, corresponding with the emergent and core selves, the child would draw upon sensory experience and the mirroring eyes and responses of those who provide primary care to construct a God-representation. For those that find a God-representation in which they can rest their hearts, in which they can believe, experiences connected with being fed, held, and nurtured, and being reflected and mirrored seem to be very important. And the opposite of that seems to be a factor in those who have a God-representation which is not nurturing and not believable.

At the period of constancy or consolidation of the self, around twenty to thirty months, we see a God-representation that in some ways replicates and reinforces the relationship between the self and the dependable objects, the dependable other persons, in one's life. The constancy that one has experienced or that one longs for with significant caretakers in one's life is projected onto a God-representation if there has been enough of that constancy to allow that association to occur. And then we begin to have a true transitional object relation to God: "I feel you are with me, even when others I rely upon are not." The obverse of that, where that kind of constancy has not been available to the child, brings consistent feelings that "I cannot feel you, I cannot feel that you are there for me, I despair." Around age four, Rizzuto theorizes that we will find a kind of objectification of God, in symbolic representations that can be idealized, so as to compensate for parental deficiencies. This makes for a more secure world in the midst of the insecurity of discovering death. We have here God constructed in terms of idealized parental images. "You are wonderful. You are the almighty," or the opposite of that. And then around five, a kind of realism about both the parents and the self emerges and God becomes less idealized. God becomes identified, in Rizzuto's view, with the experience of love and being loved or its opposite.

Some Thoughts About Infancy and "Original Sin"

In conclusion let me share some preliminary thoughts about the concepts of original sin and the fall. I would like to recall for you my claim that each of the levels of emergent selfhood is a place where worth, mutuality, respect, and the possibility of alienation are at stake. Even prior to the verbal self, it's possible that there can be insults to the core self or to the inter-subjective self. My hunch is that the roots of the alienation that comes to be symbolized and experienced at about the time of the autonomy versus shame and doubt stage often lie in those earlier senses of selfhood in what we called earlier primal agonies or primitive agonies.

The language of fallenness which we have inherited in the Christian tradition (and it may be that St. Augustine won too firm a victory over his opponents on the issue of original sin) can be enriched if we couple alongside "fall" a term that I've coined, "befallenness" (*Pastoral Care*, 103-05). Befallenness refers to those elements of weakness, of vulnerability, of propensity to alienation, that take form in us, due to circumstances utterly beyond our control. They may arise due to a family we did not choose to be born in, with its own pattern of vulnerabilities and distortion for which we had no responsibility. They may issue from the distractions, the economic pressures, the disabilities of that family unit to provide adequate care for us in that early period. Or there may have been a deficit of personal and collective faith that would have enabled them to project for us a coherent experience of the world. Any combination of those things could contribute to our befallenness. Befallenness is not equally distributed in the world. Some persons have a lot more of it than others.

Now, fallenness. At about the time the verbal self begins to emerge, some degree of conscious choice exists for the child as to how he or she will respond to the environment of which s/he is a part. It doesn't mean we have all the leeway in the world to respond any way we want to; we have that legacy of befallenness. But we come to consciousness, and we have some sense of complicity or involvement in the alienation that we experience, to whatever degree. I suggest that we begin to have a more flexible way of talking about the consequences of the fall, and recognize that a good bit of what the Christian tradition has symbolized with fallenness is *be*fallenness.

Moving from this distinction of fallenness and befallenness, I want to raise the question whether drive theory of the traditional Freudian sort and theories of infant *a'dualism* and undifferentiated relationships of the Piagetian sort aren't in some sort of unconscious collusion with unfortunate attributions of fallenness and original sin. Drive theory says that we come into the world trying to maximize our pleasure and acting on the basis of instinctual drives that are the fundamental motivations of our lives. It says that we become civilized beings only as we internalize, at great cost and with the production of great inner conflict, the restraints and constraints of the culture and society around us. "Splitness," therefore, is our inevitable heritage in this view, and the best we can hope for with the best of therapy is a kind of armed truce in which we live with that splitness. I wonder if that is not a mirror reflection of a too-harsh theological doctrine of the fall and of original sin? (Miller)

Similarly, theories of infant *a' dualism*—the view of the infant as being in an undifferentiated relation to the environment, from which s/he gradually emerges into separate being. Such theories suggest that the child is inherently egocentric and not naturally social. I wonder if here again we don't get a reification of an unfortunate and unexamined doctrine of the fall. I don't want to discard the wisdom of doctrines of original sin and doctrines of the fall; they are indispensable as a kind of hermeneutic or perspective for making sense of adult patterns and experiences. But do we not make a mistake to project those adult experiences back into infancy, creating a perception in which we predict and almost cause the very phenomena that we use to interpret our adult experiences? It seems to me that one way to understand faith is as the opposite of shame and the opposite of guilt. Early childhood faith is a kind of robust sense of being held in the care and the love of God. It arises from the establishment of what some psychoanalytic theorists call a healthy narcissism, a healthy self-esteem, a healthy self-love, grounded in our experience of the love of others.

Conclusion

It is our great privilege, as parents, as teachers and workers with young children, to be allies of the potential for wholeness with which children are created. I conclude, from this extensive examination of various perspectives on early childhood development in selfhood and faith, the following:

(1) Children are inherently social from conception, and they are gifted by our Creator—normally—with capacities for recruiting and responding to adults and siblings in relations of true mutuality. Patterns of distortion

and disease are deviations from, not manifestations of, children's potentials.

(2) Parents and other significant adults are far more important than many of us have been taught in the earliest months and years of children's lives. It is not that we imprint or mold the child, as some behaviorist psychologies would suggest. All our informants recognize that child development is a profoundly interactive matter—with the child taking a great deal of constructive initiative in our relations. But our initiatives and responses—and our provision of "holding environments" enriched with language, stories, and love—are of immeasurable importance in the development of selfhood and faith.

(3) Attention to the preverbal emergence of the different senses of self that Stern has identified may provide us with access to the genesis of some of the central dynamics of faith and religious participation. The cross-modal knowing of the infant under two months of age gives us clues to the beginnings of imagination. The generalization of interactions and construction of the evoked companion during the emergence of the core self suggest the origins of ritual and the sense of the numinous. Affect attunement in the subjective phase of infantile selfhood suggests the genesis of shared meanings and the birth of the soul. The beginning use of language and symbols in the emergence of the verbal self suggest the origins of symbolization in faith and religious participation.

(4) The account of children's composing of the image of God, drawn principally from Rizzuto, helps us to see—without reductionism—the capacities outlined in the previous point being employed to form the central religious symbol of our culture and of our lives. Her findings about the ways children's God-representations incorporate aspects of their parents' ways of being underlines the role of adults as means of grace and revelation for children. It also makes us more deeply mindful of how, in our weaknesses, neglect or abuse, we can deeply impair our children's emerging faith as well as their selfhood.

2.

The Roots of Faith: The Crucial Role of Infant/Toddler Caregivers

Alice S. Honig

Faith Beginnings

Before we can begin to examine the roots of faith in the infant and toddler years, we need to inquire what "faith" we are talking about. Shall we define faith as unquestioning belief in rituals or certain modes of prayer, certain specific gestures on particular occasions? Can we equate any one set of religious practices with early faith development? For some, faith may simply be a belief in the mysterious orderliness of a vast universe. Einstein once remarked that God was not malicious, but He was "raffiniert" (crafty, subtle). For others, religious faith may serve as a kind of payment in advance against the terrors, sorrows, and sins of ordinary lives—against a future punishment by a stern God. Some people's "faith" may lead them to condemn unfortunate others as in some way "deserving" their terrible fates. Some have believed that faith implies unswerving loyalty and commitment. Eichman, the Nazi exterminator, protested at his trial that he had only loyally and faithfully followed orders. "I gave my oath to my Fuhrer. There is nothing worse than breaking your oath." When the prosecutor asked quietly, "Even killing six million people?," Eichman fell silent.

Even those who profess moral beliefs and can reason in sophisticated ways about moral choices and issues (Kohlberg) may have difficulty in behaving morally. Everyday snobby, catty, insensitive behaviors are as common as dandelions. The psychiatrist Robert Coles, who has written so perceptively about the lives of children and of the poor, observed that:

> This is the great gap between transcendent ideologies and convictions, high-flown theoretical notions and the issue of immanence in all our lives: how we are going to behave five minutes from now with one or another person. Some people who are well-to-do, very prominent and well educated, talk a great line but don't live up to it (15).

A dialectical mystery infuses human strivings. We use our God-given energies often in fiercely contradictory yet quintessentially human tasks— the struggle for self-sufficiency and self-actualization of our personal gifts and the attempt to create empathic communications and communities with others.

The philosopher Heschel believed that *acts* of faith teach us the meaning of the acts. Purity of motive is not as important as actions. "Faith is an act of the whole person, of mind, will, and heart. Faith is sensitivity, understanding, engagement, and attachment; not something achieved once and for all, but an attitude one may gain and lose" (154). Acts of charity, consideration, small gestures of kindliness and concern, caring and compassion (in Hebrew, *mitsvot*) can define the living faith of humans. "The mitsvah, the humble single act of serving God, of helping men, of cleansing the self, is our way of dealing with the problem of evil" (377).

Perhaps most simply, then, faith is a principle of goodness that we call God (Kushner). We witness for faith as best we can in our everyday lives, giving meaning to faith as we keep the faith through our actions.

Theories and Researches: Roots for Faith Building in Babies

How are we to rear our children from birth to become members of a faith community? My assignment at the Kanuga Symposium was to review relevant child development theory and research for clues to the mighty tasks that ordinary, devoted parents accomplish in rearing babies to become helping, sharing, caring persons.

We are all meaning-makers in our world. We construct and reconstruct the meaning of our experiences. And we renegotiate our understandings as we live and learn and have further experiences to digest (Kegan). Children of despair have learned from their early experiences with caregivers the way to confusion, chaos, and cruelty. In contrast, children who have learned loving reciprocities in families can construct meanings of concern, cherishing, and steadfastness in serving God and others. They have learned faith. Who are the theorists who can guide our understanding of this process?

Jean Piaget, the Swiss psychologist, saw children as problem-constructors and as theory-builders. According to Piaget's constructivist view, children come to know the world first through actions of their eyes and hands and bodies and later through mental activities. Children create theories of logical, physical, and social relationships (Piaget). They see how the real world reacts to or intervenes in their intentions and actions. Through extension of this principle, we can see that interactions with primary caregivers are the essential ingredients by means of which young children will construct for themselves the meaning of faith. Not just what we teach, but how we teach will influence a young child's faith construction.

Imitation of caregivers who have nurtured them and on whom they are so critically dependent emerges early among babies (Bandura; Sears). Anyone who has watched a young toddler seriously sit down to read his book (upside down, perhaps) next to a beloved papa who is reading the newspaper can attest to the power of early imitations. When we watch a toddler scold and wag a threatening finger at her dolls, we know she has learned by example only too well from parents.

Margaret Mahler's theory has been particularly sensitive to the importance of the relationship between infant and caregiver. During the first three years of life, the child journeys toward internalizing a good "mother of oneness"—the term that Louise Kaplan uses in her poetic rendition of Mahler's theory. In the first months of life, the major task of the young child is to sink into an absolute conviction of symbiotic oneness with a caregiver who holds, nourishes, comforts, and ministers to the baby. Somewhere about five months of age, the baby begins to "hatch." Little limbs stiffen when baby is held; baby more and more turns outward to gaze with interest on the rest of the world. The practicing period toward the end of the first year involves lots of stretching and creeping, attempts to gain physical control over handling skills and physical locomotion.

During this period there must be a central figure to move away from. The vitality of striving to become your own self prospers if you have the conviction that there is someone there to return to if you move too far too fast—not a changing figure every day, not an indifferent caregiver who is rotating with a colleague, but a nurturing, constant one against whom the infant can struggle for individuation toward unique selfhood. Mahlerian theory talks then about the child of twelve to eighteen months pulling up to stand and beginning to toddle away into a glorious world of verticality. The toddler now has a "love affair" with the whole world. Joy and pleasure are at a peak. Toddlers at this stage are so sure that the world will hold and protect them as their parents' arms have done that they are likely to walk fully clothed straight into a swimming pool if not watched carefully!

Somewhere toward the middle of the second year of life, in the period Mahler calls "rapprochement," this assurance comes crashing down.

Greyness sets in and crankiness. Toddlers become aware of the reality that parents are not there for them exactly as they wish, when they wish. The baby's "body mind" has now become a thinking mind. Baby's struggles to become a separate person are full of conflict. It was so pleasant to be merged with the caregiver of the early months, yet it is so wonderful to be a separate, independent creature. So in these confusions the toddler becomes difficult and contrary, wanting to be separate but fearing the loss of the earlier intimacy.

Toddlers struggle toward "constancy," where the good parent who cares for you is also the bad parent who hauls you off to bed just when company is coming, or who refuses to give you a cookie just before dinner. Constancy helps us to accept the ordinary humanness of people who can sometimes be a pain and sometimes are so very dear to us. Mahlerian theory is really a tale of this dialectic dance that goes on throughout our lives— wanting to be merged, first with a loving parent, later perhaps with a beloved spouse in marriage, in sexuality, in tenderness, and as adults merged as members of a faith community in our closeness to God. And yet at the same time, there is a human streak that wants to be independent and separate. And in toddlerhood this desperate wish comes out in absurd stubbornness, as when a two year old insists on wearing his new shoes into the bathtub or tying his own shoelaces (which he cannot yet do). Tensions build and temper tantrums can storm up as toddlers struggle for control over their own bodies and behaviors. How hard it is for a young toddler even to stay still for a diaper change!

True constancy is necessary for faith development. Constancy means you can lose a job, you can lose a person you really cherish, and after mourning, pick yourself up without cursing Man or God and go on living, feeling that you will do the best you can. Constancy keeps the dialectical tensions of life from overwhelming us, helps us surmount difficulties without turning on those near and dear to us. Lacking constancy, many adults denigrate a spouse, empty their intimate other of all good qualities, and then search for another "perfect" partner or friend. Toddlers need to internalize this deep acceptance of the contradictory aspects of their strong feelings about caregivers. A well nurtured baby can achieve the "mother of oneness" within to ward off loneliness and panic and unrealistic expectations of perfection in human relationships and to preserve faith in living a fully human life serving God.

Erik Erikson's theory also offers many dialectical ideas important in quality infant caregiving and faith building (Erikson, *Childhood and Society;* Honig, *The Eriksonian Approach*). For Erikson the life span encompasses a series of eight nuclear conflicts, struggles between positive and negative (or dark) poles. During sensitive developmental periods, the outcome of one or another of these conflicts is more critical for further growth toward achieving adult identity and integrity. All the conflicts exist in some form at every stage. And each struggled-through stage eventuates in a ratio of positive to negative aspects.

The first major struggle is between basic trust that the world is a positive place to grow up in as versus a basic mistrust of caregiver and of self. When caregivers are uncomfortable or irritated by body closeness or unwilling to meet a baby's needs when the baby is upset (rather than when the adult feels like it), the child may well develop profound feelings of indifference to others' hurts. Research shows that toddlers who have been abused by parents exhibit emotional indifference toward peers in distress (George and Main).

Trust is built on a four-way signal system (Honig, *Training Infant Care Providers*). Babies come to trust their caregivers and their own needs. Parents must trust their capacity to nurture well, and they must validate and respond to the baby's strong signals of distress. Ainsworth's observations in babies' homes revealed that some babies had mothers who picked them up promptly when they cried in discomfort and tried to respond sensitively and appropriately to their babies' needs. These babies became securely attached to their caregivers. They enjoyed being held but could also accept more easily when a parent had to put them down. They cried less but used other communicative modes more toward the end of the first year of life. When the parent was present, they used that presence as a secure base from which to launch into constructive play with toys.

Building on these findings, Sroufe and his colleagues (Matas, Arend, and Sroufe) discovered that securely attached infants grew up to become more competent older toddlers. Secure children proved more positive and zestful in approaching difficult tool-using tasks. They cooperated more with parental suggestions while trying to solve the tasks. In play with peers, preschoolers who had been securely attached in infancy were more popular with peers and with teachers. In contrast, insecurely attached infants grew into toddlers who gave up far more easily when faced with difficult problem-solving tasks. They were more oppositional to parents, more negative, cried more, and threw more temper tantrums. The effects of basic trust building in infancy are far-reaching indeed.

The modalities of this first Eriksonian nuclear conflict involve a balance between *giving* and *getting*. As an infant learns to accept feeding, cuddling, and soothing in the styles the caregiver provides, and if the relationship is mutually satisfying, the child learns how to become a giver even as he or she has learned how to take in the ways and styles of the particular family. Later generosity as a participant in a faith community has its roots in the caregiving comforts and adjustments of the first years of life.

The second Eriksonian nuclear conflict has to do with a balance between achieving autonomy and a child's sense of shame, doubt, or defiance toward caregivers who try to wrest away the child's rights to have wishes and desires of his or her own. The modalities of this second struggle are between *holding on* and *letting go*. Letting go can really be explosive—witness a toddler breaking into a temper tantrum in a restaurant because a parent won't let him have a slice of bread before the meal which has been too long in coming. Toddlers can lose control so devastatingly wildly. They become so terribly upset; and if the parent also becomes upset, they will really feel life is a wreck! The best you can do for a toddler who is screaming and thrashing around is to do some deep breathing to calm yourself so that when the tantrum is over, s/he can mold back onto your body and feel that your calmness is there to hold on and to hold life together.

Letting go—of naughty words, impulsive actions, and bowel movements just after s/he has been taken off the potty—are also typical of toddlers. We must try to help them learn the differences between holding on as cherishing or defending legitimate self interests, and holding on as selfishness or uncooperative defiance. The polarities of these modalities are hard to learn. Parents would do well to remember that if too much is forced on toddlers in the way of feeding, toileting, and sleep demands, they may later reject and throw away some of our most cherished beliefs—in a reasonably clean and orderly environment, in religious observances, and social graces.

The third Eriksonian conflict has to do with using one's new-found powers of will to make choices and take initiatives, as versus a permanent sense of guilt some caregivers instill over the "creative" behaviors of young children that may cause unintended disorganizations for parents. Preschoolers are playful. They try to get others to do things for them. They play make-believe games so that parents worry whether their children are wildly imaginative or telling lies. They use intrusive modes (especially intrusions into the ears!) to talk until parents wish there were a STOP button to press somewhere.

If the early Eriksonian conflicts have been judiciously negotiated by caregivers, a child should be able to make responsible choices and, further, to take responsibility for those choices. A child should be able to hold on to his own and his family's beliefs so that he does not have to lose his identity later in a teen gang or give in to peer pressure for dangerous, self-destructive activities. Thus, fully formed faith is an adult capacity whose roots lie in early mutual interactions with caregivers.

> Out of the conflict between trust and mistrust, the infant develops hope which is the earliest form of what gradually becomes faith in adults. If you say that an adult has faith, I'd say, well, I hope so. But if you said that a baby has faith, I'd say that's quite a baby. Real faith is a very mature attitude. (Erikson, *Identity Crisis*, 135)

Ideas for Caregivers: Interpersonal Prescriptions

I believe that faith involves not only attitudes but also actions. If the creation of faith is through interactions with caregivers, then what prescriptions can we offer to help parents and others nourish faith during the infant and toddler years?

1. *Trust yourself as a caring person.* Bouts of ordinary human tiredness, angers toward a continually crying baby, or exasperation with upsets are all perfectly normal. Sometimes we want to shut the door and be free of tending to infant needs so that we can shower, read a book, make love, or just rest. Yet, despite such yearnings, we can continue to tend to baby's needs with loving care. And you are O.K. to be human in your feelings too!

2. *Trust your infant's signals.* The harmony of matching tempos and styles reassures the infant that her way of nursing, his way of wiggling while being diapered, are all right. Hurrying their bodily functions distresses babies (and other humans too!). Bath time takes longer for some. Eating is an impetuous dash and mess affair for some tots; for others, chewing and eating is a slow process that seems to take forever. Encourage a baby's interaction when the baby shows readiness for stimulation. Respect for the tempos and time needs of babies can add to their somatic conviction of worthiness. And those who feel deeply that they are worth the time and patience of caregivers can grow up with a deeper sense of meeting the needs of unfortunate people in society who need our patience and our most creative efforts in order to solve problems of mental illness, homelessness, learning disabilities, and the like.

3. *Accept the fierceness of early infant needs.* Some caregivers are startled by the fierce neediness of tiny babies (Kaplan). They may be disconcerted by how strongly babies suck, how greedily they gulp, how despairingly they cry if they are wet, uncomfortable, hungry, lonesome, or colicky. Deep inside, caregivers might wonder if a baby can devour them with such strong neediness. Some may feel they have to distance them-

selves from the baby and not respond to the almost terrifying intensity of neediness in infants. But the caregiver who maintains a sturdy faith in his/her ability to minister to needs will not tune out nor turn off. Despite the energetic expressions of distress in little ones, most caregivers with loving intentions can keep in tune with babies in the midst of crying storms. It is important not to project evil onto babies. They do not cry to hurt us. They cry as a strong signal to enlist our help for their early troubles in settling their systems (Honig, *High Quality Care*). Let us help as best we can; we cannot give up or turn away, but neither do we need to act out anger toward the tiny, helpless beings who so invade our lives with their early fierce urges. We were once babies too. Someone had faith enough that we would grow up to give to others that they were willing to be generous givers to our own early intense needs.

4. *Be generous with admiring glances and body language that affirm a child.* Admiring eyes that shine on a child help imbue that child with the energy to go on and grow up and learn all the difficult socialization skills (wiping our nose on a hanky, not on a hand; toileting rather than messing diapers; saying "please" and "thank you"; waiting for food to be served instead of banging imperiously on the table; etc.). Eyes that affirm, eyes that validate, eyes that express our belief in the intrinsic goodness and capability of baby can strengthen the baby's faith in herself or himself (Honig, *What Are The Needs?*) Early faith is woven of many strands. Faith in our willingness to meet needs has to be meshed with infants' faith in their own difficult struggles to learn, to accomplish, and to become humans who can serve to nurture others in a faith community when they are grown.

5. *Create rituals of mutuality and shared meanings with your baby.* Look where the baby gazes; comment on the toy he handles or is interested in. Mutual attention to books, objects, or familiar patterns baby prefers reinforces the conviction that all is right with baby's world. You are the special adult who knows the pattern of routines or back-and-forth games that are necessary for baby's harmony and security. Sometimes even handing a chewed-on crust of bread or a toy peacefully back and forth with

a baby is a routine that enhances baby's sense of sharing a satisfying experience.

6. *Give power to early communications.* Turn-taking talk even when infants are in the early stages of cooing and babbling is important (Honig, *Art of Talking*). Use "scaffolding talk" with toddlers whose vocabulary power may be in short supply: "We're going to see grandpa. We are going to ride in the _____." Toddlers love the power of being able to supply words. They love to name and jabber long strings of earnest syllables. Acknowledge their early babbles with your best "Unh-huh!" Expressive skills may be in short supply, but babies need to know that you respect their earliest communication efforts.

Read, read, read to babies. From early months onward, hook your babies on books. Many books for babies encourage thoughtfulness and awareness about the needs of others. Rhymes, cadenced and chanted words, and sleep-time songs will imbue your baby with delight in words and language. In order to be effective in a faith community, adults need to be able to share meanings and concerns and plans for helping and worshiping through language. Create an early passion for language.

7. *Empathize with your baby.* Empathy, or affective attunement (Stern) means being understood emotionally from your own point of view. Recognize and join in with the expression of your baby's positive feelings. But also allow your child to own his/her feelings even when you firmly disapprove of actions or words. A naughty baby, a fearful toddler, or a messy child needs to know that you understand her urges, although you cannot ever permit hurting others or things that belong to others. Researchers have found that where parents are consistent models of comforting when a baby is upset or worried and they firmly disallow the use of aggression in settling social difficulties, babies show early signs of altruism and attempts to be helpful (Pines). Such an attempt could be baby bringing his loved blanket to cover a grandma who looks tired, or offering hungry papa a taste of her well chewed zwieback.

8. *Give the gift of courage through secure, tender care for baby's needs.* Protect children from your inner volcanos of anger, from the deepest sor-

rows that invade your soul. These are your private struggles. Babies need a courageous, cheerful parent who can compartmentalize. A very depressed caregiver will have a baby mirroring the sad, depressed features within months after birth. The caregiver with many private furies will frighten the infant who sees the eruptions all too frequently. Find places and times and persons with whom you can work out private anguishes. For the young baby, courage comes from the brave model, the nurturing model, the caregiver whose cheerfully lopsided ratio of signals of approval and appreciation is far in excess of signals of anger or rejection (Honig, *Gifts of Families*). Infants reference us to see how the emotional wind is blowing, as Stern showed in his experiments with babies on a billiard table, facing a novel situation. Depending on whether the nearby parent's face expressed pleased interest or fright, the baby bravely paddled across the table or turned and scurried back in the opposite direction. Courageous toddlers are more likely to have had mothers who gave the babies control over feelings and who allowed their babies to decide the level and amount of stimulation given (Martin).

9. *Help babies build a clear sense of body integrity and abilities by providing toys and freedom to explore.* According to Piaget, children construct their ideas of how toys work and how materials feel and flow or break or topple. Physical causality, the ins and outs of space, tangible understanding of the chemistry of solutions and of changes due to mixing sand or fingerpaint are learned as little ones are given materials and opportunities to experiment. Logico-mathematical understandings of pairs or polar opposites (such as hot and cold) or gradations of heaviness, of color, of size are learned as children manipulate materials provided by thoughtful caregivers. Your wise generosity in providing materials and opportunities to build, mush, pretend play, dig, wash, solve puzzles, will allow the growing toddler to learn how the world works, just as your responsive tuned-in interactions are teaching how the world of social relationships works. The Caldwell HOME stimulation scale (Bradley and Caldwell) is an excellent tool for checking whether your caregiving, homey environment is providing enough of the interpersonal and learning experiences that help a young child develop optimally.

10. *Offer choices.* Especially in the negative stages of the toddler period, life gets rough for families and caregivers. The almost-angel baby of the past year has become a no-sayer of terrible swiftness and conviction. Yet before we can affirm our faith in the ways in which adult lives can be generative and generous, giving and sharing, we need to become separate persons who wrest for ourselves the right to say no to others' ideas, suggestions, wishes, and requests. No-saying is a stage on the pathway to yes-affirming life. But this stage is hard on caregivers. Often resentment of the toddler grows and becomes an intractable sorrow or anger invading the loving feelings that sustain adults during the myriad tasks of tending young ones. Lickona, in his book *Raising Good Children,* offers helpful ideas to cope with a strong toddler need to assert his/her own will. As you come to the corner of a street crossing with a recalcitrant toddler, you can say, "I have to hold your hand now—which hand would you like me to hold?" Or at naptime, "On which end of the bed do you want to lay down your head—this end or that one?"

Questions that alert a child's attention to relevant variables can help them make appropriate or more reasonable decisions without the fussing and fighting in which adults often become mired. The child who just wants to rush out to the yard and play—minus a jacket or gloves—needs to be asked to look outside and see what is on the lawn, and then be asked, "How will that white snow feel, warm or freezing?" And, "What could we put on our hands and ourselves to let us enjoy playing in that cold snow without shivering and getting soaking wet?" Balancing rights and responsibilities is a skillful and sometimes frustrating task for parents.

11. *Help your child learn to live within family rules.* Be firm and loving; be accepting and encouraging (Baumrind, *Child Rearing*). Have faith that although your child is different from you, your authoritative (rather than authoritarian or permissive) approach to discipline and child rearing will enhance the chances for your child to grow up to be a freely choosing and active member of a faith community. By "giving in" and not helping young ones understand reasonable rules of behavior, we take away their chances to learn to cope with frustration, to learn to find ways to fit into family needs, and to be responsible members of a household. How

challenging is the dance between "duty" and "freedom." Parenting is a hard job; high expectations and firm rules plus unconditional commitment and loyalty to children must be wisely combined in the authoritative parenting style (Baumrind, *New Directions*).

12. *Maintain your sense of humor.* Some days nothing goes well for babies or their caregivers. Tempers are frayed; disappointments are strong. A sense of humor works somewhat like a prayer. It acknowledges the impossibility of perfect adults or perfect babies or perfect days. It is a way of seeking sustenance to tide us over till better times. Faith in future harmonies, faith in the work of loving kindness has so far managed to sustain us through the difficult days. Using a whimsical sense that "Nothing works well on earth all the time" can help. Vegetables are squeezed to a mush by baby as he dives into his lunch with messing energy and sensuous enjoyment. Or a baby squeezes her banana through her fingers and proudly through her curls. Oh well, a fancy beauty salon would charge a fortune for vegetable or fruit hair shampoos or skin treatments! If a toddler is up to it, humor games can often lighten up a day. Jokes like "Doggies mee-ow" can cause grins and offer the opportunity to say "No!" to an older toddler who catches on to the game (Honig, *Art of Talking*).

13. *Help both male and female babies to become agentic and caring.* Kaplan notes that the greater activity levels of boy babies lead to more climbing and vigorous bodily movement. By such activities, boy babies define their body boundaries more clearly and often earn the admiring glances of parents who urge on their mastery experiences and victories. Little girls may not be allowed as much bodily risk-taking such as climbing and galloping. Why not?

In her thoughtful work *In a Different Voice*, Gilligan notes that there is a dialectic tension between the moral ideas of cooperation, interdependence, and the need for self-actualization. She observes that "Male and female voices typically speak of the importance of different truths, the former of the role of separation as it defines and empowers the self, the latter of the ongoing process of attachment that creates and sustains the human community" (156). In this dialogue between fairness and caring there are implications that perhaps faith may evolve differently for males and females. A conception of morality as concerned with the activity of care centers moral development around "the understanding of responsibility and relationship, just as the conception of morality as fairness ties moral development to the understanding of rights and rules" (19). Can we help both female and male infants enrich each of these strands?

14. *Crack the code of anger.* Briggs urges that we try to find the underlying feelings for our angers. None of us is exempt from anger, but often hostility is engendered by unrealistic standards for babies and young children. Sometimes our own feelings of shame or jealousy from the past lead us to strong criticism or shame of traits in our little ones that we felt miserable about when we were young. Briggs notes that "sad covers up mad" (208). If your child is too low key, without the sparkle and bounce that signals a rooted faith in family good will, then underneath there may be real feelings of resentment about too much parental control, or too many early demands for training or perfection. Children need to know they can grow at their own pace, make mistakes, and have time to become more adept. What kind of faith community can children grow up to build if deep in their hearts, they smolder with the resentment that they were never smart enough, pretty enough, or athletic enough to please their parents? If, on the other hand, you feel angry or sad, perhaps you resent "giving in" too much to your youngsters. Parents have rights, too.

15. *Lay the foundations for faith in a secure and loving God through continuity of care.* If there are too many changes in an infant's life, that baby can become terrified, acting out with psychosomatic symptoms such as diarrhea, sleep troubles, and irritation (Honig, *High Quality Care*). Find supportive others who can provide stable, consistent care for your infant if you cannot provide care continually. Frequent daily separations and changes are devastating to an infant's sense of basic trust in his/her personal community. If the roots of faith development lie in the earliest experiences of confidence in caregivers, then families must think about and feel through the implications of lack of stability and continuity in infant care.

16. *Model generosity, mutuality, and personal courtesies.* As the infinite goodness of religious faith sustains adults in their trials, children are

sustained by the memories of caregivers who were positive role models (Segal and Segal). Children are flexible. They can forgive our human foibles and failings and "ornery" times as we live through (and do not fall apart at) their tantrums and troubles. But for faith to flourish, the preponderance of a baby's experiences needs to be overwhelmingly that of positive models. That we are powerful models is certainly salient when a three year old announces, "I'm going to marry Daddy when I grow up," or in the play behaviors of children who cuddle or spank teddy bear or dolls as they are treated.

17. *Baby-proof the environment to cut down on forbidden spaces and actions.* A safe environment supports energized explorations. When curiosity is killed, a toddler's enthusiasm for learning may fade away. Sometimes children who are too dutiful feel guilty if they explore the boundaries of their own needs, their own unique gifts, and potentialities. Let the physical environment in the early years sustain early growth into the special and wonderful self of each individual child. Pots and pans can be dragged out of low kitchen cabinets for play, but cleaning agents need to be safely put away. Couches and cushions need to be tough for toddler clambering. Silk damask slipcovers don't belong in homes where babies are growing up!

18. *Accept the see-sawing needs of toddlers.* As children grow, they sometimes regress toward more immature behaviors. A toddler with a new baby in the family may ask to have a bottle. A bottle of water carried triumphantly around the house will not cripple the emotional development of your three year old! S/he may feel satisfied instead of aflame with jealousy over the sucking privileges of the new baby. If you calmly accept some regressions, some tryouts of the old ways (diapers on for tonight although baby is mostly toilet trained; a pacifier for nap because a visiting baby cousin has one), they will fall away quickly as the child forges onward toward more mature modes of behavior.

"Rapprochement" is the name Mahler gives to the toddler period where darting or dashing away often alternates with needing to fling oneself onto the caregiver for security or refuge. If we do not believe in the ultimate upward spiraling of growth, we may cripple faith development by calling toddler a "baby" for needing a lap, or we may resent a toddler for dancing away so bravely as if s/he didn't need us anymore. Toddlers are difficult to live with. They may call up the painful ghosts from our past when we were difficult babies and caregivers were furious with us (Fraiberg). Keeping the goal of faith building can help us keep our sanity and our "cool" sometimes as the (to us, unreasonable) work of toddlers defining their personhood goes on.

19. *Rethink your own parenting.* Sometimes present parenting is a powerful time to lay old ghosts to rest. Perhaps we had a miserable time of it as young children ourselves. How then can we build a firm foundation for our children's faith? Fortunately, research (Ricks) is clear that agonies from the past need not become intrusive, spiteful spirits in our own caregiving. Suppose you had miserable experiences as a child. It helps if you are indignant and even angry at the lack of nurturing you received, or if you are forgiving of the foolishness or even the cruelty of significant adults in your life. How you construe your own parents' behavior is crucial. If you felt rejected, but can accept that this early rejection is an attribute of your parents and not a reflection of your own essential worth as a person and parent, you can restore the roots of faith. A pastor or rabbi or counselor may help you in these struggles to reconstruct self-esteem. Chances are very good that you can provide a faith-sustaining personal environment for your young one with strong counteridentification rather than identification with aggression received.

20. *Reframe certain exasperating infant behaviors so you see them in a more developmentally oriented framework.* For example, Tess is dunking a piece of bread into her milk. She plunges her hand way into the glass, wetting her shirt sleeve in order to retrieve the soggy mess. As she squeezes it in her hand, her eyes widen: This sure doesn't look like the dry piece of bread still sitting on her high chair tray. Rather than interpreting this as deliberate defiance of your instructions not to mess, try to reframe by telling yourself that Tess is exploring ideas about disappearance (as the bread absorbed milk and slowly sank from sight). Her surprise is a good sign that she is making comparisons and learning about the transformations that occur when some items absorb liquid. If you reframe so that you can

understand from the child's point of view how the situation seems, you have a better chance of acting reasonably rather than out of anger. If you want such explorations to be less messy, you might plan them for bath time. But babies are messy creatures. They drip from noses and bottoms. They are sensuous and enjoy tastes and pats. Reframing can save us from attributing to babies evil intentions to aggravate or hurt.

21. *Help your baby with emotional tasks.* Babies have to learn as they grow that the person who loves and cares for them is the same person who denies them cookies just before supper, or who may take them off for a nap when they are overtired and acting out crankily. Learning to cope with the puzzle of good and bad together is hard. Toddlers need time to integrate the idea that we can manage to love someone and also resent that same person. This Mahlerian "constancy" is a long, hard achievement of the early years. Constancy is the faith that love and good feelings are still possible, deeply lodged within us. By the end of the infancy period, constancy has begun to provide the inner lodestone. Accepting the struggle of your baby learning to create constancy is a sign of your faith in the mighty forces of growth within.

22. *Find supports for yourself as a caregiver.* No one can be a giver all the time. The balance of giving and getting learned so long ago in the earliest years of life can tip to deplete any caregiver. Wise caregivers will try to find support networks, surrogate caregivers, time for personal unwinding. This may involve firm rules for a toddler's rest time even if the toddler is wakeful during that hour and looks at books quietly. You need rest times too. Nurturing the worthy person within each of us can help renew our energy for the awesome tasks we tackle daily—building emotionally healthy, joyous, people-cherishing children who will be well on their way to learning how to be positive participants in a larger community of faith later on because they have been tiny members of an ongoing faith community in the home.

Covenant in the Community: Ideas for Supporting Infant Flourishing

Beyond the principles and practices families need in rearing infants and toddlers, parents have civic responsibilities in the larger community. Here are some ideas to enhance the ultimate societal as well as personal goal of rearing young ones who can more securely take their places in a faithful society as well as family.

1. *Every public school should offer experiences which prepare its students for eventual parenthood.* In junior and senior high schools high-quality infant/toddler care centers can serve as a hub around which shop courses, English composition, and history courses can be coordinated with the experiences of students who are learning to notice, interpret, and respond contingently and tenderly to the needs of little ones. Highly trained infant caregivers can serve as excellent models and cheerful supporters of early efforts to tune in to the needs of tiny others. Bettye Caldwell has videotaped wonderful examples of fifth graders in Little Rock who became enthusiastic helpers in the care of babies as a result of participating in such a setting.

2. *Hospital or clinic based childbirth education classes should be expanded to include parent education.* Parents-to-be could learn about the characteristics and needs of babies in the first years—needs for skin sharing, body cuddling, and sensitivity to infant signals. Such ministrations ensure that the Garden of Eden is really an on-earth experience for babies long before remembrance or language can articulate such satisfactions. When suckling to satiety, pleasureful play, and sumptuous laps are the birthright of babies, then faith development can be more safely ensured as a community experience for all infants.

3. *Choices for parents who cannot or are not willing to rear a child lovingly and securely must be available.* Babies have fundamental rights to grow up in a personal community that keeps the faith with their being. When parents cannot make this special commitment, they need support for and availability of other options.

4. *Parental leave policies in industry and business that guarantee job, health care, and insurance benefits to new parents must be vigorously promoted at the legislative level.* If faith communities are not willing to advocate for children on a societal level, we will rue the results in increased mental health problems, delinquency, and school dropouts. The cost of one year in prison is far higher than the cost of supportive societal policies (Children's Defense Fund).

5. *Funding for training and remunerating high quality infant/toddler caregivers is an important obligation of faith communities.* Society is willing to put money into schools for training auto mechanics, doctors, and dentists, but infant care specialists are often recruited at the lowest wage levels. The average childcare worker in the United States has a job in the Federal Register listed below parking lot attendant! For many workers recruited to care for babies, the names Ainsworth, Mahler, and Piaget could just as well be Swiss watch brands rather than important guides to quality care practices.

6. *Preventive infant mental health facilities need to become as accessible as physical health checkup clinics.* Hot lines, drop-in centers, respite shelters, and trained neighborhood parent networks can help. "Kitchen therapy" personnel can visit homes, hear out and professionally heal and banish the sad and angry "ghosts" from some parents' past lives. Aggressive ghosts may block gentle alliances with the goodness in babies when parents, hurt earlier themselves, only perceive babies as spiteful, evil, or bad (Fraiberg).

Conclusions

Let those of us who love and work with infants and toddlers help to provide for them the nurture and guidance they need so that at the end of the infant period, the child can:

Gather and gather the strands of cherishing.
Gather and gather the voices that have been loving, playful, kindly,
    and have made them wriggle with joy.
Gather the shiningness out of caregiver eyes.
Gather the rhythms that have met their rhythms.
Gather the mutual attunements and firm, calm disciplines
    that have made them feel secure in families,
    confident of rights as of responsibilities.
And from all these hopeful affirmations, the young ones gather the
    yarns to weave themselves a coat of many colors,
    like the coat of Joseph the favored one.
So clothed, babies can grow to sturdy faith:
    —faith in themselves, in the value of their struggles to grow,
                learn, and work.
    —faith in the loving kindness of caregivers.
    —faith in the essential orderliness and friendliness of the
             universe and of Godliness.
    —faith in their ability to give generously unto others
             as they have been given unto.
    —faith in a community of service and reciprocity.

Hope and faith grow out of these subtle intertwinings of adults with infants in the early years, and the child who ends up in such a faith community knows what *being* is, compared to *appearances*.

May we all keep the faith with infants and toddlers in the first years of their lives!

3.

A Faltering Trust

Bettye M. Caldwell

The title of my presentation is obviously based upon a very famous bit of poetry. Remember the lines from William Cullen Bryant's "Thanatopsis"?

Thou go not, like the quarry-slave at night,

Scourged to his dungeon, but, sustained and soothed

By an unfaltering trust, approach thy grave

Like one that wraps the drapery of his couch

About him, and lies down to pleasant dreams.

Perhaps it seems inappropriate to begin a talk dealing with the early years of life with a quote oriented toward life's end. So, with both timidity and temerity, I offer a rewrite entitled "Genesis":

Thou go not, like a quarry-slave at morn,

Scourged to his work-site, but, sustained and soothed

By an unfaltering trust, birthright in hand,

Let faith remove the bonds of doubt and fear

And give you strength to face reality.

I take you through this little exercise with sincere apologies to Mr. Bryant, because I found in that phrase—"unfaltering trust"—a capsule statement of what faith development is all about. But a sobering reflection on the reality of life on our planet, both in our time and in most periods of history, would force us to admit that conditions seldom exist that allow its formulation. Rather, what can be hoped for at best is the phrase I have used for my title, "a faltering trust."

As evidence that it might actually be wise for children to approach life with a faltering trust, I offer four brief scenarios dealing with very real children (with changed names), all of whom are personal acquaintances of mine.

Margie is a beautiful seven year old who says she hates school and is having difficulty learning to read. One day, when she was not quite three, her mother told her at dinner time that her daddy would not be living with them any more but that he still loved her. Since that day, Margie has seen him four times for a total of about twenty hours. Her mother says she has been rebellious and difficult to control for the last three years. Margie says that what she likes best about Christmas is that she always gets a present from her daddy.

Allen, age two, was recently rushed unconscious to the Children's Hospital Emergency Room. X-rays revealed a skull fracture. Parents, both very nervous, said he had fallen from a high chair. Both were referred to SCAN (Suspected Child Abuse and Neglect), where the mother reported that the father had shaken the boy and hit his head against the wall. Father counter-charged that the mother often whipped Allen and produced large bruises.

Geraldine, weighing twenty pounds at eighteen months, weighed only two pounds at birth. Her mother was not quite sixteen at the time. The baby was cared for by a maternal great aunt for two months, at which time the mother took her back to live with her and the maternal grandmother.

After three months, the mother (then back in school) decided to release the child for adoption but refused to allow the aunt to have the baby. No adoptive home could be found and no settlement reached. Within the first year of life, Geraldine was in at least six different childcare arrangements.

Harry, age four, lives with his mother in an elegantly furnished apartment. He has a half-sister, age eight, who lives with the maternal grandmother and whom he sees three or four times a year. Twice during the past year he has been introduced to a new man who has lived in the apartment with him and his mother. He was spanked recently for telling one of his friends that the man was his daddy. He has been instructed simply to call the man by his first name and to tell people, "He lives with us."

You don't know the four children I have described, but certainly you know others very much like them. At least one out of three children will share Margie's experience of suddenly losing a father. Statistics show that following divorce in which the mother is given custody, contact with the biological father frequently ceases shortly thereafter (Gelles). Fortunately, not too many children have to go through Allen's experience. Although estimates vary (with some ranging as high as twenty percent), probably no more than five to ten percent of children experience serious physical abuse. There are, of course, those who insist that the reported cases are merely the tip of the iceberg and that the condition is far more prevalent than we are willing to admit. And, of course, little Geraldines are all too common. Young women (especially if poor and black) are at greater risk for delivering a low birthweight baby, and tiny pre-term babies are in turn at risk for physical and developmental problems. Across all social classes, one baby out of five is born into a one-parent family situation (Guidubaldi, et al). And it is difficult to know how many Harrys there are in the world. His situation merits our attention, however, as a reminder that faltering trustworthiness is not restricted to the environments of poor children.

I have described these children to serve as a reminder to all of us that the nurturance and adult responsiveness prescribed by Alice Honig do not exist for all children—or else they exist only temporarily and then are swept away in the confusion of clashing personal histories. If the foundations of faith development are laid in the family, and if the family foundations crumble for a given child, where then do we find the support necessary to help a child develop trust in the people and events in his/her world? That is, how do we help children develop trust in an untrustworthy world?

My special assignment for this conference is to focus our thinking on ways in which institutions outside the family can facilitate the development of trust, unfaltering or faltering. Obviously, such institutions have an important role to play. However, such recommendations must be based on what is known about how trust is generated and strengthened. Accordingly, a brief discussion about the development of trust is a necessary preface.

Developing Basic Trust

In several presentations at the Symposium we have heard discussions of the multiple stages that characterize the maturing of faith. Similar stepwise progressions can be observed in the development of trust. The most relevant formulation is that of Erikson, who divided ego development into eight stages, the so-called "Eight Ages of Man." Erikson's book in which these stages were introduced is now almost forty years old, and in today's world of rapidly obsolescing information, that is a long time to survive virtually unchanged. Furthermore, every new undergraduate textbook in child development introduces students to these stages and offers illustrations of ways in which the integrative achievements associated with each stage can either occur or be frustrated. In short, the Erikson formulation has profoundly influenced the way we think about the process of development.

The first thing that struck me in my rereading of this classic was a new awareness of its title—*Childhood and Society,* not Childhood and the Family as we might tend to think of it. In introducing the eight stages, Erikson indicated that he was trying to supply criteria "by which the individual demonstrates that his ego, at a given stage, is strong enough to integrate the timetable of the organism with the structure of social institutions" (246). This statement provides an effective framework for my assignment—that of considering ways in which institutions outside the family can nourish faith development and the acquisition of prosocial behavior. That is, it reminds us that all the social institutions (including the family) which play a role in the nurture of the young must somehow develop patterns that dovetail with the infant's own need system.

As is well-known, Erikson labeled his first stage "Basic Trust." Although in his definition Erikson did not quote Bryant, he might well have defined it as unfaltering trust. Let me quote a few of his words: "The general state of trust . . . implies not only that one has learned to rely on the sameness and continuity of the outer providers, but also that one may trust oneself . . . and that one is able to consider oneself trustworthy" (248). Then, after stating that fostering this basic trust is primarily the responsibility of maternal care, he quickly goes on to assert that it is the quality, not the quantity, of this care that is critical. And, to some extent, quality is determined by the degree to which the care is consistent with what is expected in the culture. To quote:

> Mothers create a sense of trust in their children by that kind of administration which in its quality combines sensitive care of the baby's individual needs and a firm sense of personal trustworthiness within the trusted framework of their culture's life style . . . . Parents must not only have certain ways of guiding by prohibition and permission; they must also be able to represent to the child a deep, an almost somatic conviction that there is meaning to what they are doing (249).

Now for one final quote—truly beautiful in both a literary and a spiritual sense—from Erikson which offers an essential reminder for all of us. In this section, Erikson concedes that the facilitation of basic trust in a child is not an easy task. He writes:

> The parental faith which supports the trust emerging in the newborn has throughout history sought its institutional safeguard (and, on occasion, found its greatest enemy) in organized religion. Trust born of care is, in fact, the touchstone of the actuality of a given religion. All religions have in common the periodical childlike

surrender to a Provider or providers who dispense earthly fortune as well as spiritual health; some demonstration of man's smallness by way of reduced posture and humble gesture; the admission in prayer and song of misdeeds, of misthoughts, and of evil intentions; fervent appeal for inner unification by divine guidance; and finally, the insight that individual trust must become a common faith, individual mistrust a commonly formulated evil, while the individual's restoration must become part of the ritual practice of many, and must become a sign of trustworthiness in the community (250).

Paraphrasing a great writer and thinker is always presumptuous, but it might be worth the risk to fit Erikson's thoughts into our own agenda rather than his. He seems to be saying that one role of religion is to offer an explanatory system that can help rationalize the occasional apparent untrustworthiness of people and events and that can help us live with a level of trust not likely to go beyond what I have called faltering. Unfaltering trust is probably quite inappropriate for any of us at any age.

Trustworthiness in the Community

Building upon these beautiful quotes from Erikson, I am now ready to offer some suggestions of ways in which institutions outside the family can help strengthen a sense of basic trust in children. The task is awesome, as the children will often be coming in contact with the institutions from family situations which are not trustworthy, as in the scenarios I related. Furthermore, some of the institutions available for the task are not all that trustworthy themselves. How many of us have had the sad experience of closing down, for lack of funds, a program which children and families had depended on and trusted? Planes do crash, and automobile accidents occur daily. Crime in the streets is a reality, and even little children are not exempt from its horrors. The outside world is typically far less trustworthy than the family.

One consequence of lack of trustworthiness in the environment is an intensification of anxiety in the individual, child or adult. This is true whether by "environment" we mean the family and home or the great outside world. And, whenever we become anxious, we become self-conscious. When our consciousness of self is too heightened, our awareness of others and their needs is diminished. Then, when that awareness is at a low intensity level, it is difficult to behave in such a way that the needs of others are accorded any legitimacy. If those who design and operate environments for young children outside the home are aware of and alert to the hazards of this sequence—environmental untrustworthiness, anxiety, heightened self-consciousness, diminished awareness of others—then certain operational guidelines for early childhood programs formulate themselves almost automatically. That is, those of us who operate programs for young children must be committed first and foremost to making them trustworthy—i.e., worthy of trust.

This obligation has profound implications for staffing and program design. Certainly it means that people and events should, in so far as possible, be predictable and should not change capriciously. People should be on duty when they are supposed to be there. Events should occur with regularity (which does not have to mean total sameness or guaranteed monotony). Emotional responses and disciplinary techniques should be those that the children have come to expect so that the affective attunement described by Fowler can operate effectively.

With this commitment to be as trustworthy as possible, the extra-home environment can play an important role in helping each child become in turn trustworthy. Every quality childhood program will list as one of its major goals the fostering of a healthy self-concept in the children. Other terms used for essentially the same objective are self-confidence and self-esteem. Without this quality, whatever else a child might have is of little consequence. A positive self-concept is closely related to trust, as with it comes the perception that one is herself or himself trustworthy. And if we are to be trustworthy, we must show sensitivity to the needs of others and assume some responsibility for their welfare—i.e., have a strong "other-concept" integrated with our own self-concept. This integration of both concepts provides direction and guidance in all our interpersonal interactions.

In our early childhood programs, we have devoted considerable effort to the fostering of healthy self-concepts in our children but generally less effort in our attempts to foster similarly robust other-concepts. This is a perfectly legitimate ordering of priorities based on personality theories such as that of Rogers. At the risk of oversimplifying complex concepts, it can be said that such theories stress the necessity for a strong self-concept as a precondition for concern for others. But in our science, as in anything else, we find what we look for and "assume that things will have had to have been" (to paraphrase Jim Fowler) as we assumed that they would be. If we are convinced that children are totally egocentric, then we look only casually for other-centered actions.

In his presentation, Dr. Fowler gave some beautiful examples of infants' perceptions of the feelings of others and the adjustment of their own actions in response to that awareness. Those of us who have worked in infant centers have received—and merited—the silent censure implied when a fifteen month old toddles over to where two adults stand discussing what is to be served for morning snack, takes the hand of one adult, and leads her over to where an eight month old is crying. Although the words are not there, the toddler is clearly saying, "Take care of him." This very young child, undoubtedly quite egocentric at other moments, is clearly demonstrating other-centered behavior. Although we have a plethora of research studies documenting behaviors (pushing or shoving, hitting, snatching a toy, etc.) that might have caused the crying, relatively little research effort has gone into the task of documenting manifestations of nurturant and caring responses from very young children (Honig).

The word that has come to be accepted as perhaps most descriptive of these behaviors is "prosocial," with "altruistic" perhaps running a close second. I like to call them "Golden Rule" behaviors; clearly they demonstrate that even very young children can treat others as they would like to be treated. The term "prosocial" encompasses behavior in which one child acts responsibly toward others by nurturing, helping, sharing, comforting, appreciating, loving—in short, by demonstrating his or her own trustworthiness as part of the existing social order.

Facilitating Prosocial Behavior in Early Childhood Programs

In this section I shall offer five suggestions of ways in which prosocial behavior can be facilitated in early childhood environments outside the home. Actually, these techniques work only in collaboration with the family, for it is doubtful that any influence on young children is not somehow filtered through behaviors and values of their families. Although I cannot cite all the available research which supports these recommendations, I shall summarize a few studies pertinent to each in order to document its validity. Some are more firmly grounded in my experiential history than in research data.

1. *Early childhood programs must be staffed by loving, trustworthy adults.* Such a statement offered as the most basic characteristic for an adult who is to work with young children is sometimes interpreted as unprofessional—and heresy for a professor of education! It could appear to minimize the importance of formal education or training. However, this does not have to be the case. What I mean to imply is that we must find individuals with this quality of loving trustworthiness and then help them get the training and experience they need in order to qualify for positions in early childhood programs.

Teachers and caregivers will not—and should not—love children as parents do. But, just as Stern can identify four different selves in infants, and just as Rubens could use fifty-three shades of pink on the flesh of the Virgin, so are there different types and shades of love, all interpretable to those to whom any given variety is directed. Montagu has described very poignantly the prepotency of love for children on the part of those who are to work with them:

The infant's need for love is not adequately satisfied unless it receives the necessary stimulations for the development of its capacity to love . . . . The child learns to love others by being loved.

Many children lead very unhappy lives, because their parents do not realize how important it is to satisfy their children's need for love, for friendship, and for stimulation. Therefore, schools should be reconstituted as agencies, second only to the home—and sometimes superior to it—for the teaching of love. The principal qualification for an early childhood teacher should be the ability to love. This requirement should stand above all others. A teacher of young children, more than anything else, must be able to love children unconditionally, to be able to communicate to them, without any patronizing and without any strings attached, that she is their friend, for friendship, it must be understood, is just another word for love (9).

The importance of this loving quality in the adults who interact with and care for young children cannot be stressed too strongly. Colleges and universities that provide the formal training needed to credential teachers of the young must be willing to develop their own selection criteria which will ensure that academic achievement does not overshadow this human component in teacher performance.

2. *The quantity of available toys and equipment and people must be appropriate for the size of the group.* The behavior of young children in groups is sometimes quite contagious. Let one little girl start a spontaneous dance, and two or three others are sure to join in. Or if one heads for the blocks, a companion soon appears. Furthermore, the children themselves will often try to set up this sort of socialized activity: "Let's go ride our trikes." Now, if there is only one tricycle, the activity is difficult to share. And rare indeed would be the child who invited a friend, "Let's go take turns riding the tricycle."

Many of the traditional early childhood teaching/learning settings can accommodate several children at once--a sand or water table, story circle, jungle gym, etc. These materials that are high in complexity invite groups of children and allow the children to interact with one another and be engaged in the same overall activity while actually doing slightly different things. For example, one child at the sand table might be pushing around or loading a small truck; another might be pressing out a line to make a road; another might be pouring sand from one container to another. Kritchevsky and her colleagues have shown that play areas containing relatively more of these high complexity materials will be utilized with less squabbling and complaining and with more truly interactive behavior on the part of young children. But even these complex play settings can accommodate only six or seven children at a time. Unless there are plenty of materials available to allow all the children in the group to be constructively engaged, there is likely to be some toy-grabbing or whining or even a push away from the table accompanied by a pious rationalization, "It's my turn with the truck."

In recent years there has been a great deal of research concerned with the importance of play and learning materials for overall development. We know that toys have an inherent attractiveness to children and their availability is associated with better cognitive development and skill mastery. Furthermore, they clearly draw children into interaction with one another and serve as a basis for the development of social skills (Bradley). In fact, when we are concerned about the effects of toys on children in groups, it is difficult to separate the power of the toys from the attractant power of the other children who might be using them (Moore). Even toddlers seem to have a concept that the sharing of toys is reciprocal. Although they cannot verbalize their strategies, their reasoning seems to go something like "You've shared with me, so I will share with you." If, however, only one child of a pair has a toy, spontaneous sharing is not too likely (Levitt, et al.). Most toddlers will then share if encouraged to do so by an adult. However, if they do share, they expect the same type of response should the situation be reversed.

Over the years I have visited some centers in which there was a dearth of play materials and have watched to see how the children cope with such a situation. Obviously they improvise creatively—making horses out of sticks, buses out of match boxes, airplanes out of paper, dolls out of ears of corn. But they also, under such circumstances, do a lot of aimless running (with or without accidental/on purpose bumping into someone else), lolling around, just looking at what is going on, thumb sucking. Once in Guatemala I visited a Servicia—rather like a parent-child center in this country—in which mothers were taught how to prepare nutritious food for their children and in which the children themselves were fed one major meal a day. There were about forty children present ranging in age from about eight months to four years. After their lunch, all the children who could walk were put out in a fenced play area and given the Servicia's only toy, one ball. The bigger and more competent children grabbed it happily, calling "Pelota, Pelota" (ball) as they ran around either throwing or kicking it. From time to time some of the smaller and less competent children would try to join in, mostly imitating the behavior of the abler children. But the fast movers—those who seemed to feel that they best understood how the ball was to be used—pretty well controlled the situation. After a while, the children who couldn't get into the action gravitated to the chain link fence and just stood there watching cars go by. After about a half hour of this, one of the adult workers came out and tried to organize the children into a game with the ball. But by then it had lost its appeal for even those who had been able to control it.

This is obviously an extreme example, for rare indeed is the center that will have only one toy for forty children. However, we have all seen the scenario played out with slight variations in settings in which there are not enough materials, or a sufficient variety of activities allowed with the available materials, for the number of children in the group. It is conceivable that this economy of scarcity is sometimes set up deliberately in order to encourage sharing. With young children, it simply does not work that way.

3. *Prosocial behavior must be modeled by the important adults in the child's life.* Most of us want our children to learn to live by the Golden Rule—at least up to a point. And we want to live the same way ourselves. However, in our interactions with our children, we sometimes operate by the rule of "Don't do as I do, but as I tell you to do." And in some cir-

cumstances that is undoubtedly not only an acceptable but a necessary rule—as when the parent engages in an act requiring far more ability and judgment than the child possesses. But when it comes to such things as concern for others and compassion and altruism, adult demonstrations appear to be far more powerful than verbal teachings and forcefully issued commands.

In a series of research studies done a number of years ago, Bryan and his colleagues demonstrated effectively the importance of modeling on the encouragement of altruistic behavior in young children. In laboratory settings, which are usually somewhat contrived and not true to life, they found that the modeling of generosity was a more powerful determinant of children's generosity than was "preaching" about the importance of sharing.

Some investigators have attempted to go beyond narrow laboratory settings and examine the effects of different types of encouragement of prosocial behaviors in the real-life environment of an early childhood program. One of the better known attempts along these lines was made by Yarrow, Scott, and Waxler. After providing careful training to caregivers in ways of modeling sympathetic and helping behavior, they observed young children's behavior in their groups. Two weeks after the specific modeling had occurred, the children showed more sympathy and helping behavior in settings quite different from those used in the training sessions.

An important question to consider here is whether training provided in one setting will influence behavior in a different setting—i.e., whether there is transfer of training. Perhaps of particular interest to parents is the question of whether training provided at home will influence their children's behavior in church or school or childcare programs. Hoffman and Wundram asked parents to describe how they had taught their children to share. Some parents indicated that they did this by taking toys away if their children did not share; others stressed taking turns with subsequent deprivation. A few parents indicated that they taught sharing by demonstrating sharing to their children—e.g., providing cookie cutters for the child while making cookies, giving the child some safe tools with which to work while the parent was using tools, etc. Children whose parents had shared with them, thereby modeling the desired behavior, were more likely to share with other children at school.

Important modeling is also provided by children for one another in early childhood programs. Parents often worry about that, fearing that their children will pick up bad habits from other, less well behaved children in the group. Interestingly enough, there is relatively little evidence that this sort of negative modeling has much effect on young children. The reason for this appears to be that children who are aggressive and disruptive have low status in the group. The other children do not like them and avoid contact with them. Moore suggests that by such cues the children "nudge each other toward maturity" (107). On the other hand, children who are relatively more socialized and who are group leaders often "earn" that status by exhibiting more prosocial behavior such as helping and sharing. Other children imitate them, perhaps because the more prosocial children are obviously successful and the imitators themselves want to gain more influence and status in the group. Whatever the mechanism, it seems to work and to help all the children learn that prosocial behavior will, in the long run, meet their needs better than antisocial and egocentric behavior.

4. *Prosocial behavior must be valued and reinforced.* This principle is so obvious, so generally accepted by parents and teachers, and so adequately supported by research evidence (Honig) that relatively little discussion is needed here. However, in spite of the general acceptance of the principle, we sometimes tend to forget it. Many parents who understand the importance of reinforcement of behavior they want to encourage in their children will still occasionally slip into the pattern of commenting on behavior only when they want it to change. Yet a quiet "I was so proud of you when you let Timmy play with your cement mixer [a special favorite] when he was here today" will help to lock that pattern of sharing into the repertoire of possible future responses.

It is possible for teachers in early childhood programs to encourage thinking about prosocial behaviors while, at the same time, reinforcing with attention and praise children who demonstrate or report such behaviors. The best and most consistent examples of this type of reinforcement that I have ever seen occurred in the kindergartens of the People's Republic of China. In the kindergartens (for children ages three to six) as in all of their schools, what the Chinese call moral development is always listed as the top priority of the program (Kessen). Intellectual and physical development are presumed to be of less importance. With kindergarten children, moral development essentially boils down to prosocial behavior—helping others, sharing, not thinking of the self first, showing respect for elders, etc. The importance of behavior falling into this category was stressed in every aspect of the curriculum—language lessons, themes of little songs and playlets, story books, art productions, sessions of what they call "productive labor" (which may involve having four year olds wash the cups used by the three year olds in the school), and on the playground. One of the best examples of adult reinforcement of such behavior occurred in the Chinese version of "Show and Tell."

Visualize the following scene. About thirty-five three year olds are seated in little chairs arranged in the shape of a horseshoe. The teacher stands in the open end where all children can see her with an easel holding a set of posters that depict the following series of events. A little child who is playing ball drops his handkerchief. Presumably the handkerchief is now dirty, having hit the ground. Another child, playing nearby, picks it up. But before returning it, she takes it home and washes it! In the last scene, she hands it to her friend, all neatly folded. Although there are no words on the posters, you know the little boy is saying, "Thank you very much."

The story alone is enough to blow the mind of a Westerner. We are likely to say to ourselves, "That will never sell in my classroom." But what is important in relation to this principle of the reinforcement of prosocial behavior is the way the teacher used the story. After having two or three children come to the front of the room and retell the story to the group (the language lesson), she then called on the children to hold up their hands if they had done anything during the week similar to what the little girl in the pictures had done. Several hands went up, and the reports were fairly stereotyped and undoubtedly reflected things the children had heard before—giving up a seat on the bus to an older person, helping their mothers clean the apartment, helping someone across the street, etc. It is entirely possible that none of the children who responded had ever actually done those things. What is relevant is that they were reinforced (given attention) for at least being able to verbalize a behavior pattern that showed concern for others.

Certainly creative teachers in our own early childhood programs offer similar attention and praise for manifestations of prosocial behavior. What is significant here is that the teacher set up a situation that would enable her to reinforce at least the idea of prosocial behavior in the children in her group. We are quite likely to capitalize on spontaneous manifestations of such behavior and praise it. However, in American "Show and Tell" times, we often encourage children to focus upon themselves as they show a special possession or tell about an experience or achievement. Teacher behavior that will foster self-esteem in the children is critical, and there is no intent to belittle such efforts. The point is that there is room for both in the early childhood curriculum. If the teacher reinforces prosocial behavior in the children, those who learn such behavior will in turn come to be regularly reinforced by friendly encounters with the other children, which will invariably lead to better self-concepts. Thus, teacher reinforcement of prosocial behavior will indirectly reinforce self-esteem in the children.

5. *The facilitation of prosocial behavior should be part of the curriculum as well as a cornerstone of program philosophy.* Just as there are curriculum units aimed at facilitating language and math development in young children, there are a number of specific programs that have been designed to facilitate prosocial rather than antisocial behavior in young children. Relatively few of these are directed to children younger than kindergarten age, as much child development theory has encouraged the point of view that very young children cannot be expected to engage in much prosocial behavior. But, as indicated above, one reason such behavior has not been found is that it has not been looked for. Relatively few of these programs have been taken through rigorous steps of program design, field testing, modification, and evaluation. A typical procedure is that someone comes up with a good idea, tries it out in his or her own early

childhood setting, persuades a few other people to try it, and then may or may not find a publisher and distributor. Once published and in the public domain, its success depends less on valid evidence of effects than on the number of people who can be persuaded to try it because it "looks good and makes sense."

One of the best known of these packaged programs is DUSO (Developing Understanding of Self and Others), developed by Dinkmeyer. The acronym by which the program is known is also the name of the dolphin hand puppet through which many of the ideas are communicated. Wearing the puppet and guided by prepared scripts, the teacher presents ideas which help the children verbalize their feelings and accept and understand that other children have the same feelings and desires. Songs, story books, role-playing, and games that come with the materials help foster the development of positive self-concepts and find good qualities in other children in the group. Although there are many teacher testimonials of the value of the program and studies showing improvement in self-concept in first and second grade children (Martorella), its effectiveness with younger children has not been subjected to independent evaluation.

My colleagues, Phyllis Thompson-Rountree, Mark Cooper, and I (Elardo and Cooper; Elardo and Caldwell) developed a human relations program called Project Aware for the elementary school with activities beginning at the kindergarten level. Objectives of Aware are similar to those of DUSO—to help children become aware of their own and others' feelings and to encourage them to find prosocial action alternatives when in conflict with other children and adults. Again, data pointing to positive benefits were more impressive with upper level elementary children (fourth and fifth graders). Many teachers who participated in the implementation of Aware felt that the manual did not offer enough activities appropriate for kindergarten children.

The prosocial curriculum with perhaps the most coherent theoretical underpinning and certainly with the greatest amount of evidence of effectiveness is the PIPS (Preschool Interpersonal Problem-Solving) program of Shure and Spivack (*Interpersonal Problem-Solving*). This approach is based on the assumption that cognitive mediation is a vital part of conflict-avoidance in both children and adults. How children think is as important as what they think in determining their actions. The PIPS strategy involves three major skills: (1) helping children develop the ability to think of alternative solutions to interpersonal problems, (2) consideration of the impact of one's actions both on oneself and others, and (3) learning to specify means-end relations—i.e., the number of steps and the length of time necessary to reach a goal. These thinking skills are deficient not only in young children but also in older children and adults with a variety of psychological problems.

A typical training program using PIPS involves three months of daily twenty minute, teacher-initiated lessons which are like riddles and games. Pictures, puppets, and stories are presented which depict interpersonal problem situations, and the children are asked to think of all the ways that the child in the picture could handle the problem. The strategy is to encourage thinking of multiple approaches, so no particular response is rewarded. In all the activities, the children are encouraged to think about what would happen if they took a particular action.

Research evaluating the effects of this program has been uniformly encouraging. Four and five year olds from both advantaged and disadvantaged backgrounds and with a wide range of IQ have been shown to improve in thinking skills following their participation in this program. In addition, they have been found after training to be less impulsive, less demanding, and less emotional when frustrated (Shure). Furthermore, and most significant, these gains held up for at least a year after training. The authors have also taught parents to use these techniques with equally encouraging results (Shure and Spivack, *Problem-Solving Techniques*).

The last curriculum to be discussed is somewhat different from the others, twenty episodes of *Mr. Rogers Neighborhood*. Certainly the producers of this program and the parents who encourage their children to watch it think of it as fostering prosocial behavior, and certainly we know that children will imitate behavior they see on television. However, there is always a question as to whether the passive learning typical of television viewing is as effective with young children as any sort of teaching situation would be which allowed children to respond to the people and ideas involved. Friedrich-Cofer and her colleagues designed a study which would not only evaluate the effectiveness of the programs but would also determine whether there is added value associated with hands-on use of materials such as those depicted in the programs and with the provision of training for teachers of ways to extend the concepts represented in the programs.

Their research was done with over one hundred Head Start children ages two to five in the Philadelphia area. Children in a number of centers were placed in one of four groups. One group watched twenty "neutral" television programs. One group watched the twenty *Mr. Rogers* episodes. The third group watched the *Mr. Rogers* episodes but had free access in their classrooms to many replicas of objects depicted in the program—stories that repeated the messages, puppets and picture books, clothing like that worn by the TV characters, props similar to the backdrop of the programs, etc. The fourth group had everything that the third group had, but in addition their teachers received twelve hours of special training to help them learn how to reinforce ideas presented in the programs and how to use the program-related materials.

Results showed significant effects only in the third and fourth groups. There were no differences between the children who viewed the neutral programs and the *Mr. Rogers* programs on such things as imaginative play, positive interpersonal behavior, and self-regulation. However, on most of the measures used in the study, the groups that had access to materials which they could use and that received special teacher training did differ from those who only watched either the neutral or the *Mr. Rogers* programs. The authors felt that the big difference came with the addition of the play materials which allowed the children to role play and re-enact the themes from the programs. This research offers an important lesson to all who would use television to foster prosocial behavior in young children: find some way to put into the hands of the children replicas of materials used in the programs so that the children can "rehearse" the positive behaviors they have seen characters in the programs carry out.

There are many more of these prosocial curriculum units than can be discussed here. An interesting thing is that these approaches have come from a variety of settings, some of them seemingly quite different from one another: religious education (ranging from archly conservative to quite liberal), humanism, the peace movement, moral education. Yet in spite of these differing philosophical origins, they are all strikingly similar. All basically want to help young children feel good about themselves, accepting this as a necessary precondition for feeling kindly toward others. Most are concerned with helping children find and learn to think of non-violent alternatives that can be used to resolve conflicts. All deal in some way or other with the necessity for social cooperation as a foundation for group living. And most support modeling and reinforcement as ways of encouraging such behaviors. In short, all try to communicate to the children that the world around them can be trusted if they will learn to act in such a way that others find them trustworthy.

Epilogue

It is difficult to summarize everything I have tried to share in this paper. As a personal note, when I prepare for a verbal presentation or write for a journal or book, I often write the summary as soon as I prepare an outline. That way, as I develop my thoughts, I know what it is that I have to have said.

Not so this time, for my preparation of this paper has been as developmental as the progress through time of the children we wish to serve. Only now, having said and written it, do I know just what it is that I said and wrote.

In view of my heavy reliance on Erikson at the beginning of this presentation, one might well predict that I would turn to him for a quote to wrap up my thoughts. Not so. Rather I have chosen a line from the poet Sara Teasdale which to me encapsulates a child's faith better than any other I can think of:

And children's faces looking up,

Holding wonder like a cup.

"Holding wonder like a cup!" What a magnificent phrase. We have all seen it in our own children and in our work with other people's children. In that sense of wonder we see the nascent faith of little children. We see it communicating:

> There is so much I don't know that you know, but I trust you to help me learn. I trust you to help me cope. I feel the majesty of this universe and realize that I am a part of it. I also trust it—that universe—and expect it to be believable and understandable, manageable and trustworthy. Right now my trust is in you and it is unfaltering, but your imperfections and the exigencies of life will cause that trust to falter. But I believe that you can help me work it out. And when you don't know all the answers, I believe that you will call on a power and a knowledge greater than your own to help us. I believe. I trust. I have faith.

A lot to be communicated in one look of wonder, one might say. But in our lives with children, in or out of the home, we are blessed with far more than one look of wonder. Those looks shine on us every day and give us a chance to shine back our responding message of trustworthiness. That is our main responsibility to young children in their quest for a faith to sustain them in their lives—to be as trustworthy as we can, to help them become continually more trustworthy themselves and, with the power for good that comes with being trustworthy, enlarge their spheres of concern to take in others in their family, their daily lives, and the entire world.

4.

Attitude Education in Early Childhood Faith Development

Lucie W. Barber

All of us came to the Kanuga Symposium because we want the very best for young children. Jim Fowler's contribution has been a theory of faith development. His research helps us better understand early childhood as a precursor or foundation to a lifetime task of making meaning of ordinary—and extraordinary—life events. Alice Honig has helped us consider caregiving practices which parents use to nurture faith in their babies. Bettye Caldwell drew our attention to the antecedents of concern for others. We have talked about the bad things that happen to little children as well as the good things, and we have spoken about justice and advocacy. How can we improve the condition of the youngest members of our communities—the communities of family, neighborhood, daycare, school, church—that make up our nation? How can we go about the nitty-gritties of providing the very best for young children?

My contribution is to try to answer that question by talking about education—education for the children's parents and teachers and for the children themselves. I will be talking about a specific kind of education, religious education. Furthermore, I will be talking about attitude education as the religious education which is appropriate for early childhood.

Religious Education

Let us back up for a moment to religious education in general in order to lay some foundations for attitude education. You have all heard of religious education so I am on firm ground there. If we start with the familiar, we can see where attitude education fits in.

A currently popular device is to classify religious education into various models or approaches. I will mention one of these efforts from the 1980's, although I will use only her titles, not her interpretations. Here are the approaches described by Sara Little, of Union Theological Seminary in Richmond:

Information-Processing

Group Interaction Models

Personal Development

Indirect Communication

Action/Reflection

Let us look at Information-Processing for the preschool child. The title reminds me of the teapot, the teacher, pouring information into the cup, the learner. You and I know that education at such an early age doesn't work that way. Information gets poured in, all right, but the processing is not adult. In Piagetian terms, the child is preoperational. In Goldman terms, the child is prereligious. Perhaps it is more useful for us to realize that young children just don't think like adults. Information-Processing of the adult type does not seem to apply, but let's not throw this model out entirely. Young children can memorize prayers and catechism as readily as they can spew forth complicated TV commercials.

Moving on to the Group Interaction model, religious education proceeds because persons interact together, discuss together, and learn through social interaction. This is a good way to learn, but does it apply to preschool children? I think not in the same way as with adults. Babies and toddlers with limited mobility hardly move from group to group. Very little so-called discussion is possible. Two and three year olds move, but socially they do little beyond parallel play. Children four through six move like lightening, but how much can they learn from groups when they are still so bound up in themselves? We are talking now about the very beginnings when egocentrism gradually fades over many, many years. Let's not throw away the Group Interaction model yet, but it's not going to be much help for the infancy and toddler years.

Now we come to the Personal Development model of religious education. What does this model have to offer for the religious education of preschool children? In this sort of summary glance at today's religious education, I would say that the Personal Development model has a great deal to offer. However, some cautions are important. Who are the educators? Who are the learners? The Personal Development model can be truly important when the learners are the teachers. Mark me well here. The learners are the parents and teachers of the preschool child. Developmental theories paint the early childhood years in mysterious ways. Listen to some of Jim Fowler's appellations: "primal," "pre-language," "intuitive-projective," "episodic experiences," "imaginative." Parents and teachers must learn to understand little ones if they in turn can truly teach religion to our youngest.

I will be coming back again and again to the Personal Development approach as we proceed. As I have said, I am trying to lay a foundation for attitude education at the preschool level. Do not forget developmental theory.

Indirect Communication is Sara Little's next approach to religious education. Please pay a good deal of attention to this category because I am sure we all resonate to the power of symbols and symbolism in religious education when we talk about what impacts on young children. What we are talking about here is the aesthetic approach—music, color, pageantry, poetry, the whole appeal to the senses. You have heard the label "sensory-motor." What really gets to the children gets there through their senses and through their bodily actions. This approach is important in children's religious education, and I plan to get back to it as we head into attitude education.

I just made a connection between Indirect Communication and children at the sensory-motor stage. Perhaps you still expected me to be talking about religious education for adults. As we talked about the approaches of Information-Processing, Group Interaction, and Personal Development, I did not entirely write them off for children. I am gradually leading up to the fact that religious education is one thing for older children, teens, and adults, and quite something else for early childhood.

The final approach, Action/Reflection, is certainly an adult category. Adults need to try a behavior in religious living, reflect upon it, and learn. However, they can do just this in their approach to children, and they can help the children do the same. Consider the eighteen month old who shoves the particle of cereal off the high chair tray and intently watches where each crumb lands. Messy as all get out—yes—but isn't that action-reflection for learning?

What I have been trying to do is to take a look at religious education today to see if it measures up to our needs in this symposium on early childhood. I have pointed out five categories of approaches to religious education and suggested that the approaches are really adult-oriented, not oriented to early childhood. But I have not turned aside from any of the models. I am laying foundations for attitude education which is going to incorporate and build upon those adult models. But attitude education is going to "fit" the children.

Attitude Education—An Introduction

Attitude education, naturally, is all about the teaching and learning of attitudes. An attitude is defined as "an enduring, learned predisposition to behave in a consistent way toward a given class of objects" (English and

English). We will be talking about attitudes where the class of objects is religious. More specifically, we will be talking about attitudes for faith, or at least the foundational attitudes for faith. There is a prevalent myth that attitudes are "caught," not taught. I am not denying that attitudes are caught, or taught unintentionally. Perhaps that is what socialization is all about. What I am saying is that attitudes can also be taught. Attitudes can be taught intentionally, systematically, and in a manner where the results can be evaluated. These are markers of education. The caught myth leaves us high and dry on intention, system, and evaluation.

The idea that attitudes can be taught in an educational setting may be new to some of you. Actually, attitude education has been around for a long time. I will go back to 1935 in this country when Ernest Ligon founded the Character Research Project at Union College in Schenectady, New York. In the first half of this century, character building and religious education were almost synonymous. The word "trait" was used for attitudes then. The traits came from Ligon's interpretation of the Beatitudes in the Sermon on the Mount. Through an extensive psychometric testing program, Ligon ordered the attitudes possible at different age levels which progressively establish such mature traits as mercy, forgiveness, compassion, and sacrifice. In other words, Ligon started with mercy, forgiveness, and so forth; and then through testing hundreds of children of all ages, he found the precursors at each level. These precursor attitudes were the basis for Ligon's Research Curriculum (Williams and Greene).

I came to the Character Research Project in 1964 when the strategies for teaching attitudes were well established for children in nursery school through senior high school. I spent eighteen years at the Character Research Project, the last ten as Director of Applied Research. A great share of the research and program development was devoted to the early childhood years, and from 1969 to 1982 we worked on the birth to thirty months attitudes.

Remember what I said earlier: In attitude education you begin with the mature attitude and trace back through the developmental levels to the possibilities at the level where you plan to teach. Here are the mature attitudes for faith with which I worked in the 1970's: "Trust in a God creator and the self-confidence to accept God's grace." What are the precursors to trust and acceptance at the preschool level?

In *The Religious Education of Preschool Children* (25-34), I espoused the following precursor faith attitudes. The young child should learn to:

1. Trust those who love and care for him/her

2. Appreciate nature

3. Appreciate the predictability of events

The first goal of trust in caregivers is a precursor to trusting in God. Appreciation of nature and the predictability of events are precursors to accepting God's gifts. Small steps, but nonetheless important first steps on a life-long progression to mature faith.

Of course, the educational goals for the child may indeed require some learning goals for the parent or teacher. The child cannot learn to trust unless the parent or teacher is trustworthy. The parent or teacher may need to learn to appreciate nature if there is going to be any chance for teaching the child to appreciate nature. Finally, a home or classroom with scheduling chaos is no place to teach anything about predictability of events. Parents and teachers must provide a secure, predictable environment. But if the parent or teacher is well prepared, the child can learn these precursor attitudes for developing faith.

Mature faith cannot be achieved without mature hope and mature love. Therefore, in preschool religious education we must consider precursor attitudes for hope and love. I have dealt with these elsewhere (*Religious Education*, 35-53), but an overview might be helpful in suggesting the scope of attitude education.

Mature hope can be defined as "Reliance on the Kingdom of God now and hereafter and trust in the potential for obtaining greater knowledge and understanding of the unknown." At the preschool level, children can learn:

1. A positive attitude toward life

2. A joyful attitude toward learning

The educational goals for a positive approach to life involve the elements of dealing with frustrations, coping with fears, and expressing cheerfulness. The educational goals for the joy of learning include purposiveness, persistence, and creativity.

Loving God and loving one's neighbor are required of all Christians. Mature love is inevitably related to mature faith and mature hope. The three traits belong together. But we can unravel the precursors of love by teaching little children:

1. Positive self-regard

2. Positive orientation to others

Both these educational goals are precursors to loving one's neighbor as oneself. Both, in turn, are prerequisites to loving God. The chained relationship goes from Love of Self—→ Love of Others—→ Love of God. God's love for each and every individual connects the link of love.

All of these precursor attitudes can be taught at the preschool level. The question of how to teach attitudes comes next. We will begin with a brief introduction to the principles of attitude education.

The Principles of Attitude Education

These eight principles of attitude education are basic rules to follow if you want to be effective at the preschool level. I have grouped these principles into three categories, the first two of which lead up to category three, the actual teaching-learning moment. Here are the principles and their categories:

Principles	*Categories*
1. Uniqueness of the learner	Background for the
2. Research the learner	Teaching-Learning Moment
3. Assesses the learner's developmental level	

4. Step-by-step procedure Planning the Teaching-
5. Build on strengths Learning Moment
6. Goal setting

7. Provide a stimulus Teaching-Learning Moment
8. Provide a reinforcement

We will be looking closely at each principle. But in this overview, please notice that in the first category, the focus is on understanding the learner, that is, the individual learner. This is a practical suggestion in the family. It gets more difficult in nursery school with multiple learners, but it can be done. Also notice that the three principles in the first category are interrelated. Research is necessary in assessing developmental level and in determining uniqueness. However, this is the kind of research that comes naturally to the loving parent or teacher. We will speak more about this kind of loving research as we move along to specifics. Notice too that the first three principles relate to all the other principles. The first category is called "Background for the Teaching-Learning Moment" because we want this kind of religious education to fit each one of our precious children. We systematize but we do it lovingly and with understanding of the child.

Before we leave this brief overview, I want to dispel a possible misunderstanding about attitude education. This has to do with the third category where the principles are "Provide a stimulus" and "Provide a reinforcement." In old-fashioned learning theory terms, this looks like the $S \longrightarrow R$ paradigm of association by contiguity. "Learning...consists of the formation of some kind of hypothetical connection in the central nervous system between an S (a stimulus) and an R (a response)" (Bugelski, 38). This makes us remember Pavlov and his salivating dogs and Skinner and his black box. It makes us cringe about "conditioning." I am realistic about conditioning. Conditioning is going on just naturally and at random all the time. The baby cries (S); the baby is fed (R). The baby learns to associate crying with a drink of milk. Sucking the thumb or a pacifier is associated with some comfort from distress. A behavior is learned.

There are some parent behaviors which come quite naturally and which also condition the toddler. How about parents who yell when their small explorer darts into the street? The yelling is aversive reinforcement to the darting child, to be sure. Nonetheless, the parent does know best about safety in traffic, and the child's risk-taking behavior must be extinguished.

Let us be quite clear about the differences between Watson's and Skinner's behaviorism and another term, "behavioralism." Behaviorism is basically S—>R. Certainly I am aware that Pavlov's conditioning was classical conditioning, which is quite different from Skinner's operant conditioning. Certainly I am aware of primary and secondary reinforcers in early learning theory. But essentially the —> between the S and R was the "black box." Behaviorists deal with a one to one relationship between a stimulus and a response. Data from experiential or introspective sources are worthless to a behaviorist.

Behavioralists, on the other hand, are extremely interested in that arrow. This is the social science approach to education (Lee, *Content of Religious Instruction*). Education becomes an art-science. The teacher must monitor the learner, the environmental variables, the subject matter to be taught, and the goal to be achieved all at the same time. The goal is a desired behavior which can be evaluated. Thus, the "behavior" in the term "behavioralism." But behavioralists are not behaviorists, and let's be clear about that. Behavioralism is much broader and all-encompassing than behaviorism. Attitude education belongs to behavioralism. That is the reason for principles 1-6. That is the reason why loving research adds the nurture dimension to attitude education. Perhaps the art-science aspect will become clearer as we go along.

Now let us begin to paint the picture of the art-science attitude education by taking a closer look at each of those eight principles. I will take the first of the educational goals for preschool faith development, "Trust the caregiver," to illustrate the educational process.

Uniqueness of the Learner

The best kind of education is personalized to the individual learner. I would expand upon that by suggesting that religious education must be personalized to the individual learner or it isn't religious. Particularly in religious attitude education, the uniqueness of the learner must be appreciated in order for a teaching-learning situation to be effective.

Here, for example, is a father trying to teach four year old Lisa to trust him and his ability to help and guide her. As one of many, many lessons, the father chooses a lesson in helping Lisa learn to ride her new bike. But Lisa is not just any four year old. Lisa is a fiercely independent little creature, a dare-devil of the scariest degree. Another part of her uniqueness is that she loves animals more than most little children. Lisa's dad wants to guide Lisa to become a safe bike rider. But she is so independent that it is difficult to get her to accept any guidance, which is part of good trusting. He uses his knowledge of her great love of animals.

Lisa's dad sets up a practice bike-riding session by telling Lisa a story about little animals who are scared of a bike-riding giant who might hurt them. Then Dad has to cross his fingers and hope that Lisa demonstrates some care in practice which he can reinforce. He has made his lesson on trust fit Lisa's uniqueness. But the teacher, Lisa's dad, can only learn about his daughter's uniqueness by researching the learner, Lisa.

Researching the Learner

Researching the learner is a keystone principle in attitude education. It relates to every other principle. It is essential to attitude education as an art-science. But we are not talking about cold, laboratory research. We are talking about warm, loving research. The parent or teacher observes, perhaps even records behaviors, and then plans a teaching-learning situation. If the chosen, desired behavior results, the parent/teacher reinforces that behavior. If the desired behavior does not result, it is back to the drawing board again to plan a stimulus that better fits the learner. The reinforcement must also fit the learner, the unique child, because proper reinforcement will encourage the behavior being repeated and thus learned.

Let's return to Lisa and her father. The father researched his daughter so that the bike-riding lesson fit the child. He went to all that trouble because he loves his daughter and wants to give her his very best. That is why we call it loving research.

Assess Learner's Developmental Level

Part of the teacher's research involves assessing the learner's developmental level. Since fitting the teaching-learning moment to the child is so important, it helps the teacher to have an understanding of child development. Knowledge of levels of development provides a kind of scaffolding upon which to build so-called lessons. Assessing levels systematizes the whole venture.

I have found that five developmental levels are useful during early childhood. The titles will give you clues to the contents of each level.

Newborn

Infant

Toddler

Run About

On Beyond

It is hardly necessary to describe these levels to this audience, but it is important to point out that the progression from Newborn to On Beyond is a progression from least mature to most mature for a preschooler *in the attitude under consideration.* It is also important to note that the contents of each level are behaviors readily observable by parents and teachers. I will illustrate with Lisa and her dad more about assessment devices as we move on to the next principle.

Step by Step Procedures

A prevalent mistake that is made by many adults is to insist upon mature behavior from immature children. Expecting mature behavior is unrealistic and it is harmful. What an awful burden to put on a child! How much better to proceed step by step and expect only what is realistic.

Now we go back to Lisa and her dad and an assessment device for the attitude, "trusting the caregiver." The Newborn behaves in a trusting manner most of the time unless there is colic or messed-up diapers. But the Newborn has no other choice since s/he is so entirely dependent. That's not trust, but foundations are laid as the baby's needs are met (Erikson). The Infant makes great progress as people and objects are distinguished. Neither of these levels applies to four year old Lisa. Her father reads on at the Toddler level. He reads about the battle between dependence and independence as mobility and language increase. This sounds like Lisa, our fiercely independent four year old. He reads on at the Run About level. Lisa can dress herself, take care of the bathroom routines, and play with other children. This sounds like Lisa too. He also notices that the Run About level includes the behaviors of asking for parents' advice, training, and guidance (Barber and Peatling). Here is where Lisa needs strengthening. She is entering this level, but she certainly is not at the On Beyond level where the most mature preschoolers are learning that there are adults other than parents whom they can depend upon and trust.

You can see that an assessment device gives Lisa's dad a scaffolding to help him see where Lisa has been, where she is now, and where she will be going. It helps him proceed step by step in a realistic manner. It helps him systematize his teaching. His next step is to build on strengths.

Build on Strengths

Lisa's dad has decided that Lisa needs to learn to come to him for advice and guidance in learning how to ride her new bike. You will remember that part of her uniqueness is her love of animals. He told her a story about little animals who were afraid of a giant bike rider. He was building on Lisa's strengths.

So much of preschool religious education starts with the question, "What is wrong with this child?" Trying to correct what's wrong has many pitfalls. Certainly parents and teachers must correct what's wrong if the child's safety is involved. A child who darts out into traffic must be corrected, but it does not make the child or the parent feel very good when yelling or spanking is used. And aversive reinforcement is not as effective as positive reinforcement. Ask the question, "What's right with this child?" and build from there. Parent reports received through the years at the Character Research Project have demonstrated that building on their children's strengths works. When children feel good about what they can do well, undesirable behaviors gradually melt away.

Goal Setting

We are now getting very close to the teaching-learning moment. The background research has been done lovingly. The direction of progress has been ascertained. The strengths of the learner have been recognized. What is the behavior which is the desired result of the teaching-learning moment? What is the goal?

There are some markers of a good goal. First, the goal must be an observable behavior which the parent or teacher can reinforce when it occurs. Next, the behavior must be something attainable by the child. Expecting Lisa to ride "no-hands" in these early bike-riding lessons would be a very poor goal. And finally the goal must be specific, naming time and place. Specificity is a help to the parent or teacher. A vague goal allows the parent or teacher to procrastinate and possibly weasel out entirely. A specific goal pins down the parent or teacher.

Now let's look at the goal Lisa's dad recorded:

On Friday afternoon as soon as I get home from work, I will help Lisa ride her new bike. I will hold onto her as much as she needs while I tell her about the frightened little animals. If she lets me help her instead of pushing me away, I will praise her. If she says, "I do not want to hurt the little animals," I will also praise her.

The goal is specific, naming time—Friday after work—and place—home. There are two goals which are observable behaviors—allowing her father to help her and saying, "I do not want to hurt the little animals." Both behaviors are attainable by four year old Lisa. The stated goal also mentions the last two principles, providing a stimulus and providing reinforcement. The father is going to help her and tell her the story—the S—and the father is going to praise the desired behaviors—the R.

Providing a Stimulus

Now comes the teaching-learning moment. Providing the stimulus is the well planned lesson which fits the learner. Lesson is perhaps a misnomer at the preschool level. Lesson suggests the schooling model. Actually, a great deal of preschool attitude education occurs outside a classroom. The lesson Lisa's dad has planned is going to occur on the sidewalk in front of their home. The teaching-learning moment can be planned in the home, in the park, in the playground, at church, at the library, or in most any location. Of course, a teaching-learning moment can be planned for a nursery or daycare classroom. The principles still apply, and each teaching-learning moment must be planned for each individual child. The challenge for the teacher is enormous, but it can be done. This has been demonstrated in Sunday Schools where Character Research Project lesson plans have been used in nursery and kindergarten classrooms.

Providing a stimulus, a lesson, is like setting up an hypothesis. If X (the stimulus) is provided, then Y (the goal behavior) will occur. If Y does not occur, or, to put it another way, the hypothesis fails, what happens? Nothing. Lisa pushes her father away, rides like a demon, runs over caterpillars, scares the Jones's cat, and crash-lands in Mrs. Lowbottom's hedge. Her dad must swallow his pride and his rage and ignore the results as best he can. Lisa must not be reinforced for undesired behavior. Obviously the stimulus he provided did not fit Lisa. More loving research is called for. But if behavior Y does occur, the parent or teacher provides reinforcement.

Provide Reinforcement

Just as research is required in setting up a teaching-learning moment which is appropriate for the unique learner, research is required for providing the appropriate reinforcement. Hugs and kisses do not reinforce Lisa—she squirms free. But Lisa does like praise and stars on her chart. Eddie is reinforced by a pat on the shoulder. Jennifer feels good when she receives a marble for her collection. Each child is different. An approving grin from the teacher is enough for Mike. Whatever makes the learner feel loved, respected, worthwhile, and special will reinforce the learner and cement the learned behavior.

A Picture of Attitude Education

This has been a whirlwind journey through the principles of attitude education. Perhaps a picture or diagram will be helpful. We have been talking about attitude education as an art-science. Each principle is a piece in a jigsaw puzzle. When we get the puzzle all put together, we can see the picture. Here now is my attempt at the picture of what the parent or teacher does in this art-science which is attitude education at the preschool level.

The parent or teacher is represented by the outside circle. The learner is represented by the inside circle. The learner is involved in the learning moment and, of course, the behavior or goal. The rest of the titles, the principles, are parent or teacher activities. The teacher sets up the environment. The teacher lovingly researches the child. You can see Category One of the principles at the top of the large circle. Research, Assessment of Developmental Level, and Uniqueness are long-range planning—the loving research that goes into understanding the learner. Category Two

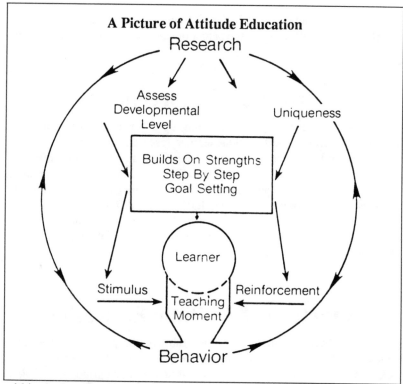

A Picture of Attitude Education

within the box contains the immediate planning of fitting the lesson to the child. Then comes Category Three, the teaching-learning moment which funnels into a behavior. Note all the arrows. They move toward the teaching-learning moment. However, if the resulting behavior is not the desired behavior, the whole research cycle begins again. It looks complicated; but once you get into this dance of an art-science, it gets easier and easier. I believe it is the loving research and the growing understanding of the child that makes attitude education so worthwhile, plus the fact that teaching becomes more and more effective. When you work within an orderly, systematic educational system where results can be evaluated, you feel you are doing your very best for these smallest of our children.

With that introduction to attitude education, I would like to go on to more specifics. I want to talk about strategies in attitude education and then about research in this type of religious education before I conclude this discussion.

Strategies in Attitude Education

By strategies, I am talking about the pedagogical practices the teacher or parent has available. It's like the tools in a tool box. A tool box loaded with tools does not get the job done unless each strategy fits the child, the unique learner.

Storytelling

I am starting with a favorite strategy, particularly with preschool children—storytelling. I recommend storytelling highly. However, there are caveats in attitude education. While I do not disagree with the proponents of the enculturation approach (Westerhoff) to whom telling the story is so important, I wonder if they have asked themselves these questions: "Does the story fit the child? Is the child at a developmental level which suggests that the child can understand the story? Is the story the stimulus for the child? Or is the storyteller the stimulus? Does the storyteller plan to reinforce desired behaviors?" The list of questions could go on if the parent or teacher is playing the art-science game of attitude education. But let me suggest a procedure for using a story as the stimulus at the teaching-learning moment (Barber, *When a Story Would Help*).

1. Decide upon the general attitude you want to teach.

2. Pare down that attitude to your child's developmental level. Not an easy task but with your knowledge of child development, you can do it.

3. Pick a story to illustrate the teaching point you wish to make. This applies to a fantasy story, a Bible story, or whatever you choose.

4. Choose the desired behavior you seek from your child that will help you evaluate results.

5. Make your story fit your child and thereby stimulate your particular learner to demonstrate a new behavior related to the attitude.

6. Tell your story; and if the desired behavior occurs, reinforce the learner appropriately.

I assure you that when you become practiced in attitude education, you can follow this storytelling procedure with no difficulty at all. Do it by the recipe a few times—it feels awkward at first but comes to flow naturally like any new skill.

Modeling

Now we come to identification theories. According to some learning theorists, the learner identifies with a model because the model reinforces the learner. According to the developmentalists, the learner is motivated to retain the love and approval of the model who has the power to control rewards important to the learner. The psychoanalysts explain a process whereby the learner identifies with a rival who receives rewards the learner wants (Lee, *Content of Religious Education*).

Any way you look at it, conditioning is involved. Once the conditioning is understood, modeling can be used with the principles of attitude education. But it must be carefully orchestrated to the particular child and behaviors must be reinforced. Socialization theories are unfortunately vague when it comes to modeling. The learner mysteriously "picks up" imitated behaviors. But we can do better than that when we use a modeling strategy along with other strategies in the art-science of attitude education. And we can know what we are doing because we can evaluate results.

Let us look at some examples of modeling in attitude education. Here is a mother whose two year old son needs lessons in becoming a family helper. The mother, as part of her daily routine, sweeps the kitchen floor. The little boy has his own little broom. He also has his Family Helper poster displayed prominently on the refrigerator door. If the little boy imitates the sweeping behavior, the mother reinforces that behavior. This particular little boy is pleased by a star on his Family Helper poster.

Then again, we can look at five year old Jennifer. She is one of twenty children in kindergarten. Jennifer adores her teacher, but she does not adore one of the youngest children, Kenny. Kenny is a rambunctious child who kicks down other children's block towers. The teacher must help Jennifer stop beating up on Kenny. The teacher takes Jennifer aside and tells her, "The next time Kenny ruins your tower, I want you to watch what I do with Kenny. Then maybe you can treat Kenny the same way." This is modeling with a little explanation. Since Jennifer adores her teacher and looks for guidance, the strategy might just work. If Jennifer imitates the teacher, she can be reinforced. If this modeling strategy does not work, the teacher can use other strategies in her "toolbox." But in each case the lesson is individualized to Jennifer. The lesson must fit to be effective.

The next strategy looks like modeling but there are distinctions.

Role-Playing

I hesitate to use the term "role-playing" because you may misunderstand my use. Role-playing is defined as "A method for teaching principles affecting interpersonal relations by having the subject assume a part in a spontaneous play" (Hilgard, 631). The definition does not get in our way. However, the prevalent use of this strategy occurs with promoting attitude change in youth and adults. The learner plays a role—not the learner's customary role—in order to see what it feels like to be in someone else's shoes. This often leads to attitude change (Lee, *Content of Religious Instruction*). Now we can understand that preschoolers find it very difficult to appreciate someone else's feelings (Cooney and Selman). Most preschoolers are still locked into egocentricity. Therefore this is not the type of role-playing we are concerned with here. The role is carefully chosen ahead of time by the parent or teacher so that it fits the child, the child's situation, and the child's strengths. And of course the role behaviors can be reinforced when they occur. Here are two examples of this strategy, one at home and one in nursery school.

Kaitlynn is a mature four year old who loves people. She seeks guidance from her mother because she wants to be prepared for tomorrow's guests. Her Mother says, "I can help you. We will act out some of the things now that will happen tomorrow. You play the role of hostess, and I will pretend that I am a guest. You can greet me at the door, you can show me where to put my coat, and you can pass the food. We will make a play out of it so you will know just what to do."

How about fifteen children in a nursery school? It is not difficult to pick a role, hostess, which fits Kaitlynn. But picking a role for fifteen children! The teacher and aides have to do some preplanning for this adventure. The lesson attitude is "Developing the self-confidence to participate in social groups" (Hampson). Through their loving research of each child, the teachers have gotten to know their children. What roles can they choose which will fit each child and help each child feel self-confidence? There is the role of Learner. Curious Kenny, Linda, and Eddie fit this role. They can be reinforced when they learn to put together the new puzzle or play with the new learning toy. "Kenny, Linda, and Eddie are learners. We are glad they are in our class." There is the role of Helper. Jennifer, Manuel, Rita, Shawn, and Peter just naturally like to help. When each picks up or helps a younger child, a teacher can say, "—is a helper. We are glad s/he is in our class." Brian is the oldest in the room. He is picked for the role of Leader. When he shows Julie, the smallest and quietest, how to wash her hands, a teacher can say, "Brian is a good leader. Julie is a good listener. We are glad they are in our class."

You could finish off this example with the five remaining children. Pick a role to fit each child which will promote the child's self-confidence. Watch carefully for role behavior and reinforce that behavior. If you are successful, you wind up the day with each child learning a small bit of the attitude "self-confidence in social groups." You will have engaged in attitude education.

Of course, if the teacher is not successful, it is back to the drawing board again. The role did not fit the unique child. The role was beyond the child's developmental level. The teacher did not give the child enough help in performing the role. The classroom situation did not give the child the opportunity to play the role on this particular day. Perhaps the child wasn't feeling well, or a pet puppy at home died the night before.

Any good teacher looks at all these factors and plans accordingly. Nonetheless, there is an educational system in attitude education. And with a system, the teaching-learning situation can be analyzed for successes and failures. Evaluation can take place. That is why I move now to discussing research in attitude education.

Research in Preschool Attitude Education

Since assessment of the learner's developmental level plays such an important part in attitude education, I want to describe the seven *Scales of Self-Regard* (Barber and Peatling). You will recall that the parent or teacher must assess the learner's developmental level *in the attitude being taught.* The Character Research Project (CRP) wanted to help parents teach their preschool children attitudes for positive self-regard. Children must be able to love themselves in order to love others and ultimately to love God. Working from a theoretical model of integrated personality which specified seven components of Self-Regard, we developed the Barber Scales of Self-Regard. Here are the scale titles and their associated behaviors:

We worked from the literature on child development and from the hundreds of parent reports on their children's behavior available at CRP. Once the painstaking task of scale construction was completed, field testing began. There were three field tests, the first in Indianapolis with 150 participants and the second involving 125 parents across the nation. The final field test involved mothers, fathers and teachers from Episcopal schools across the country. In this national sample, 125 children were rated with the Barber Scales of Self-Regard and, unlike the other samples, with the Minnesota Personality Profile II and with SCAMIN, a well known self-concept measure. By the end of 1975, CRP had 2940 completed Self-

The Seven Barber Scales of Self-Regard

Scaled Title	Behavior
Purposeful Learning of Skills	A child in order to feel positive about self must behave with a purpose
Completing Tasks	A child in order to feel positive about self must behave with persistence
Coping with Fears	A child in order to feel positive about self must learn behavior skills for coping with fears
Children's Responses to Requests	A child in order to feel positive about self must decide to trust authority and behave cooperatively
Dealing with Frustrations	A child in order to feel positive about self must learn behavioral skills for dealing with frustrations
Socially Acceptable Behavior	A child in order to feel positive about self must behave in a manner acceptable to others
Developing Imagination in Play	A child in order to feel positive about self must learn creatively about his or her environment

Regard Scales available for analysis. The published manual for the Scales reports on usability, validity, and reliability in extensive detail. We had accomplished what we set out to do—constructing useful scales for parents and teachers to assess developmental levels of children in attitudes contributing to positive self-regard.

The next step was to build a parent education program around the scales. The *Realistic Parenting* program was carefully built to show parents how to engage in attitude education with their preschool children. The program was successfully tested in Ohio in 1978 and published in 1980. To be sure, the program needs to be updated with today's technology of audio-visual capabilities. However, what we are looking at here is the research that can occur in attitude education because we are dealing with an educational system that is orderly and intentional. I want to illustrate by describing the research for two doctoral dissertations. The first is by Brenda Rambo at George Peabody College for Teachers, Vanderbilt University, in 1982. The purpose of her study was to compare one of Tennessee's "model" preschool programs with a church-sponsored, daycare program. Both programs were located in the same homogeneous community in south-central Tennessee. The model program was a carefully planned, progressive education program; and the daycare center offered custodial care but no educational program.

The Barber Scales of Self-Regard were used as a measure of self-concept along with the Preschool Self-Concept Picture Test. The Barber Scales were rated by each child's mother and teacher, and the Self-Concept Picture Test was administered to each child by the teacher. This was a control group, posttest only design, with 30 children in the model program and 26 in the daycare. Would the children in the model program have higher self-esteem in the spring than the children in daycare?

Rambo did not find significant differences with the Barber Scales, although she did with the Picture Test which favored the daycare children as having higher self-concepts. However, there were serious flaws in the research design, as the author admits. For example, the model program children spent three hours a day in school whereas the daycare children spent up to nine hours a day. One interesting result was that mothers with children in the model program rated their children higher on every Barber

Scale than did mothers of daycare children. Does the model program affect mothers or affect children's home behaviors positively?

Comparisons were made between groups with the Barber Scales, but I would suggest that the Scales can also be used intragroups. For example, in the model program, teachers rated the Scales Children's Responses to Requests and Dealing with Frustrations much higher than the Scales Purposeful Learning of Skills and Coping with Fears. The Scales can be used to evaluate strengths and weaknesses in an educational program.

The next illustration from doctoral research is Doris Blazer's study for the University of South Carolina in 1981. Blazer adapted the *Realistic Parenting* program to Sunday morning adult education meetings in Episcopal churches in the Southeast. There were five experimental groups of mothers and fathers of 24 children who worked with the program from September through December and three control groups with 21 children who were promised *Realistic Parenting* in the spring but who did not meet in the fall with the parent education program. Parents completed questionnaires on demographic variables. The experimental and control groups were well matched although there was not random assignment to groups.

The 85 parents of both groups, experimental and control, rated the 45 children on all levels of Self-Regard Scales two times. The first ratings occurred in early fall before the parent education program began in the experimental groups. The second ratings occurred six months later but before the control groups began *Realistic Parenting*. Since random assignment to groups was not possible, analysis of covariance was used to control for any initial differences in the children. "Comparison of the adjusted posttest scores revealed significantly greater six months' gains in positive self-regard scores by children whose parents had participated in the parent education program" (Blazer, 106). Although there were many other findings in Doris Blazer's study, the point has been made that with the orderly, systematic approach of attitude education, sophisticated research is possible.

From Osmosis to Order

Now I want to conclude this presentation on attitude education at the preschool level with a few remarks to summarize where we have been and where we can go with attitude education. I was intrigued by the title of a recent book, *Loving Your Child Is Not Enough.* I have not yet read this book; it is only the title that catalyzes me. I believe that loving your child is good and beautiful, but it is not enough. We can do much better. We can research the learner, learn about the child's uniqueness, and assess developmental levels of our young learner. Then we can set a goal in a step by step procedure which builds on the child's strengths. And finally we can provide a stimulus and a reinforcement which fits the child. And we can do all these things lovingly. But love all by itself is not enough.

As I read so many books by religious educators who want to help parents with their children, I constantly run into words like "instilling," "impacting," "forming," "identifying" and the like which are somewhat nebulous. Here's another phrase that makes me uneasy: "She will come to know...." Yet another phrase is "without any direct teaching." How will the child "come to know" "without any direct teaching"? The child may, indeed, come to know. That is hit or miss, random, and often pure luck. I call that natural seepage the "Osmosis Theory." I think we can move from osmosis to order by engaging in attitude education at the preschool level. We can use an educational system of demonstrated effectiveness and thereby put our energies into an orderly teaching-learning program. We can move from osmosis to order as we do our very best for our youngest learners.

One of the benefits to learners in attitude education is that children brought up in the system eventually become self-motivated learners. The goal of self-motivated learners is the ideal of every educator. Religious educators particularly want self-motivated learners who will continue lifelong learning of God's gifts and God's will for their lives. Love of learning is an attitude the foundations for which are set in very early childhood. In attitude education more than self-motivation to learn is involved. The self-learner must research self in order to appropriately self-stimulate and self-reinforce. I am going to use the term "intrinsic conditioning" to refer to conditioning coming from within (Barber, *Religious Education of Pre-school Children*, 80-83).

We at CRP found over the years that parents whom we trained in attitude education soon began to use the principles on themselves. This was particularly true with *Realistic Parenting*. Parents set goals for themselves as they set goals for their children. Furthermore we encouraged parents to talk over the child's goal with the older child. Parent and child became partners in the process. The child was beginning to learn intrinsic conditioning along with the parent.

Let's take another look at Sara Little's approaches to religious education. The first approach was Information-Processing. Wasn't Lisa processing information about little animals as she rode her new bike? Wasn't Katilynn processing information about the role of hostess? The second approach was Group Interaction. Certainly the nursery school children were engaged in this approach as they learned positive attitudes about participating in groups. The Personal Development approach is the basis for the principles of assessing developmental level and proceeding step by step. But eventually children can learn to be realistic about what they should expect of themselves. The Indirect Communication approach is valuable for teachers and parents of our very youngest. Aesthetic stimuli to the senses is the major approach for adults to use with children before language is well in place. However, there does come that time in the mid-preschool years when pride in achievement begins the process of the child motivating self. Beginning steps, to be sure, but all important in fostering eventual intrinsic conditioning. Sara Little's final approach is Action/Reflection. The rudiments for action/reflection are present in the second year of life. We build on them by providing appropriate reinforcement for desired behavior. But eventually the child can provide his or her own rewards. You and I self-reward constantly—at least I know I do. Coffee-breaks are self-rewarding for work accomplished. Dining in a restaurant is a favorite reward for me. Shopping rewards many. A self-served snack rewards children after a long day at school.

The point I am trying to make is that we can use all of Sara Little's approaches to religious education within the system of attitude education. The attitudes we teach must be positive, and they must be realistic for the child. But at the Run About level of development, when children seek advice and guidance, we can begin to draw them into the system of attitude education. We can begin to talk with them about goal setting and evaluation. We can engage in laying foundations for their own intrinsic conditioning.

The art-science of attitude education is not for the purpose of making slaves of children conditioned to carry out our wills. The purpose of this art-science is to give children freedom. As children move toward autonomy, they can take over their own learning as they develop more and more mature and positive attitudes of faith. That is good religious education.

I have just one final thought for concluding this presentation on attitude education. That thought has to do with the proactive nature of attitude education (Barber, "Proactive Religious Education"). We should proact rather than just react as we do our best for our youngest children. Michael Zelden, a well known Jewish religious educator, has pointed out that so much of religious education is reactive, a reaction to the environmental situation. How much more effective to plan ahead of time how to forestall and prevent destructive attitude formation! How much better to promote positive attitude formation in the crucial early years. We do not have to wait pitifully for bad things to happen. We can get in there fighting on God's side. We can proact in religious education. The educational system of attitude education can be our highway to a better future for the youngest learners who are in our charge. Loving research and conditioning toward freedom are our possibilities for the future of faith development in early childhood.

5.

Strengthening Families for the Task

Kevin J. Swick

A very clear message emerged during the many sessions of the Kanuga Symposium on Faith Development in Early Childhood: Strong families provide the foundation for meaningful faith development experiences. Presentors' sessions as well as Covenant Groups and Special Interest sessions were alive with ideas about various aspects of the family's contribution to the faith development of children. What are some of the things that happen in families that are critical to the faith development of children and their parents? Insights from our discussions on involving parents in their child's faith development were expressed in many ways.

My memories of closeness and warmth in our family are, to me, the vital pieces of "family" that no other group can fulfill.

It was our helping each other, even when we disagreed, that made me see the "family" in us.

The putting to work of our religious ideals made us aware of how important it was to live faith and not just talk about it.

It's a spiritual dance that happens—parents loving infants in
a way that no other person can replicate.

Families provide the vital ingredients for forming spiritually rich
relationships. The warmth and acceptance that can occur in family interactions are the substance of faith development during the early years.
Mutuality experiences that occur in the family—e.g., teaming, celebrating,
forgiving, supporting—serve to "seed" the family's involvement in the
faith development process in positive directions. Unfortunately, as many
Kanuga participants noted, it is the absence of attributes like warmth, acceptance, and mutuality in families that has taught us their significance.
Recent findings that detachment patterns formed during early childhood
have a lasting influence throughout the life-span certainly add further support to the significance of faith development in families during the child's
earliest years (Burchard and Burchard; Spivack and Cianci; Magid and
McKelvey).

Our analysis of family life in today's society revealed many influences
that may be eroding the ability of parents and children to function as a
loving, supportive unit. In particular, we identified an over-emphasis on
material values, rapidly changing social roles and customs, unrealistically
high expectations for the parenting role, lack of support for families from
business and government sectors, and inadequate time and resources to
engage in family living as a meaningful journey. But participants felt
strongly that there is a spiritual dimension to parenting which is absent or
unresolved for many:

> Learning to deal with one's self as more than just one is very
> threatening. I find many young parents attempting to struggle with
> this without much guidance. I suspect many family pathologies
> are rooted in our lack of spiritual insight on who we are and what
> our mission is.

> The awesome feeling of being a parent was both exciting and
> scary; this sense of power creates a real need for "becoming more
> adult." My interactions with today's parents force me to realize
> they are not finding the time and room to sort through this process.

Knowing one's self as good and vital to the world is prior to all else. Faith in "self" as spiritually vital is the link to becoming a growing parent. Without a trust in self that is real and growing, parenting loses its integrity.

Learning to "become more adult" and to be sensitive to one's growing spirituality is difficult in our culture because of the devaluation of childrearing and family life. At Kanuga we recognized the complexity of parenting and the need for seeing parenting and the faith development process within a broader framework. Two dimensions of this broader framework we explored were (1) the need for a spiritually based understanding of parenting, and (2) the need for a more just and spiritually supportive societal context for family life.

When we talked of children and faith at Kanuga, we consistently centered on parents as the primary influence on children's faith development. It is through parents' everyday actions and explanations that children make meaning of their experiences and learn who they and others are. For example, the abilities to love, to share, to solve problems, and to see one's self as valuable initially develop within the parent-child relationship. As "faith educators" parents are engaged in establishing a secure and loving environment, sharing themselves intimately, protecting their child from danger and abuse, projecting an enlightened view of faith-filled living, and engaging others in growth experiences. In effect, the loving things parents do with and for their children are the roots of the child's early faith. In Westerhoff's view, we come to serve as each others' witness in a compassionate and just sense of our destinies.

We repeatedly asked ourselves: What is it that parents are or do that enables them to be effective in their role as "faith educators"? Responses centered around the following attributes: they have positive self-images; a spiritual awareness is reflected in their daily living; an orderly and planned system of human growth is evident in their lives; a clear sense of "teaming" exists in the marital relationship; they show love and caring openly; and a sense of inquiry, growth, and commitment is evident in family relationships.

But what seemed most significant was parents' awareness of their own spiritual lives, their understanding of the parent role in spiritual terms, and their ability to draw upon the faith community's resources to meet their family's faith needs. These parents seem to create an image of parent firmly grounded in Westerhoff's view of vocation: "For most people, *vocation* means merely *career,* but to the Christian, vocation is first and foremost our response to God's call to fulfillment" (72). In order to become a parent who can serve as his/her child's faith educator, one must first have a sense of one's personal essence—one's goodness, value in the eyes of God, and potential for spiritual growth. Becoming a "spiritual self" and a parent are integrally related; both efforts are part of the faith journey and serve to strengthen each other. Having an image of one's self as a spiritual parent is not an easy process; it demands engagement with both the physical and spiritual realities of life. It is not simply carrying out a series of activities; rather, it is an active effort to construct a coherent pattern of values, understandings, and behaviors whose consistent application sets the stage for family faith development.

Becoming a parent is a process which begins long before the child is born or conceived. This process begins in our images of being a parent. Parents form images by calling up the past, drawing from their significant experiences, and creating scenarios of what can or might be. Imaging is the tool we use to form mental and spiritual maps for use in our parenting actions. This imaging process is most intense just prior to and during the initial period of parenthood, and parents continue to use these early images as their framework for action over the family's life-span (Galinsky).

Any parent whose images are devoid of the spiritual center that bonds parenting to the faith journey is likely to miss the vocational essence of being a true "sponsor" in Fowler's sense (*Stages of Faith*). In fact, it is in the effort to fulfill one's vocation as sponsor and shepherd that parenting becomes real. Parent images of warmth, trust, nurturance, mutuality, growth, and renewal are rooted in their faith histories. These faith images serve as the foundation for faith actions and are actualized in various ways—parent-child warmth, marital harmony, and spiritual growth. At Kanuga many Covenant Group discussions included personal reflections on how parents had positively influenced us through their faith commitments. Their daily prayer, service to others, sensitivity to our development, and courage to grapple with life's complexities were some of the faith actions which made lasting impressions. Such nurturing actions not only seed human bonds but can also act as a halo over the life-span of children and parents.

In a society where parenting and other nurturing roles are devalued, it is essential that the faith community lead parents toward a realization of their spiritual leadership in the family. Parental self-insight is the beginning of the family's faith journey. It is the commitment of one's "Christian presence" to sponsoring children:

> Christian presence in the world requires the ability to pay close attention to every aspect of life. Only when we listen can we properly respond to what God is calling us to do. When we have the courage to listen and the insight to respond, then things begin to happen. We discover, for example, that we can be agents of transfiguration far beyond our limited capacities and vision (Westerhoff, 80).

The faith community's role as sponsor begins with fostering parents' spirituality as a way of signifying the importance of their commitment. This specialness is symbolized in the formation and articulation of a theology of family, celebrations of life that show the central role of the family in faith development, and community rituals where children are welcomed into the family of faith, such as infant dedication or baptism, or a service of thanksgiving for the birth or adoption of a child. The image of parent as a spiritually growing person can be strengthened in various ways: providing premarriage education on the essence of marriage and parenthood; sponsoring study groups; offering worship and educational experiences directed toward the parent image-making process; conducting pastoral visits to new parents at the hospital or home; and promoting enrichment and renewal experiences such as special prayer sessions or retreats. Other important forms of support come in offers of assistance by friends in the faith community, development of foster grandparent programs, and the creation of a Hot-Line for emergency care.

A form of social and spiritual re-bonding occurs among new parents and their significant helpers. It is a way of personalizing the symbolic baptism through real actions as parents who can grow with the love and care of others. Having access to friends who support but avoid smothering is certainly one of the hidden links to the trust-building that parents must carry out in their daily actions. A "psychology of faith" emerges in parents as they experience rituals, spiritual growth, and social specialness. Kanuga discussions often centered on the need for parental self-esteem. One seminar participant related how her personal struggle with "becoming adult" was enhanced by friends in the church. "It was like a vitamin shot—an injection of pride." And Galinsky emphasizes that the parent-helper is most influential through validation of the person's inherent worth and potential for growth.

As faith educators parents play many roles. At the beginning, *nurturing* is the most important role. It is an embracing of the child that begins in the intimacy of parent-infant bonding and extends throughout the family's lifetime. The joyful warmth, care, and support parents share with infants and young children serve as the spiritual energy for the family's journey. This nurturing must be a part of the family's living faith, evident in marital and friendship lives as well as in parent-child interactions. As many Kanuga members observed, the early signals of a "faltering trust" occur in the erosion of caring within the marriage relationship. In ministry and in community support work, a renewed focus on marriage relationships sensitizes couples to the significance of nurturance for all family members.

A second major role parents play is in introducing their child to the larger world as they *choose and design experiences* appropriate for the child's growth. Two functions parents carry out in this process are the *development of a positive guidance orientation* and the *creation of an interpersonal support system* that nurtures total family growth. A positive guidance focus is based in warm, sensitive, and nurturing family living. The distorted notion that control emanates from rigid parent expectations and behaviors was countered by Alice Honig's observation that trust-building is interactive; it blossoms within gentle and responsive relationships.

The heart of any guidance or control process is support. Family support begins with parents or, in the case of single parents, with close adult friends. The internal support of family helping roles and other enabling behaviors strengthens the total foundation of faith development. The building of trust and mutuality through close, loving relationships provides the family with a center of spiritual and emotional security for growing in their faith journey. Expanded support in the form of help and validation from the faith community broadens the family's source of strength and thus increases its potential to pursue the faith journey in meaningful ways. The challenge faced by parents is to orchestrate, experience, and guide this process toward a spiritual perspective.

The "faith living" that parents project through their pattern of everyday life events and activities is an important dimension of this process. At Kanuga we took note of many such actions which may seem small but which serve as the energy source for positive family relationships: family walks, evening or morning prayer, "talk times," job sharing, and recognition of one another as special people in the eyes of God. Initially parents are the pace-setters in designing these faith nurturing experiences, but gradually the process becomes a shared venture where children are taken into the planning and doing. Faith teaching, in the early years, is more than anything else a process where parents and children bless each other with many experiences of trust, love, and mutuality.

Two special and vital ways parents actualize their faith educator role are in *helping children come to know God* and in *establishing a family pattern of involvement* in the life of the faith community. Through family prayer and celebrations of birthdays and special family events, as well as in church or synagogue activities, children receive their initial impression of God. And, as a part of family involvement in religious services, fellowship, and ministry activities, children come to feel at home within the larger family of faith in which they participate. Children's images are indeed primal, and powerful, in serving as the base for further growth in their understandings of self, others, and God. Central to their understandings are the feelings conveyed to them through all experiences: parent nurturance, church celebrations, community caring, and welcoming embraces that come through gentle, trustworthy relationships with significant others.

While individual members can contribute to the nurturance of young families, it is essential for the faith community to sponsor parent support projects that bring faith development closer to the home by encouraging home-based prayer and action-discussion sessions. These early support experiences serve not only to validate parents in their special mission but also sensitize them to the process of helping their child come to image himself as a Child of God. We at Kanuga found few resources which help parents introduce children to God and to the faith community in appropriate ways. While much has been written for Sunday School teachers, we feel strongly that family activities, church practices, and outreach ministry efforts need to be oriented toward the goal of strengthening parents' spiritual growth and understanding of the vocation of parenting.

But parents must reach out too! Growth occurs where sharing and helping are part of an ever-widening circle. Families need both their own unique identity and a broader vision of their place in the global faith community. This can be achieved through something as simple as sharing a meal and an evening with a family we know but really don't know, or inviting an "unchurched" family to accompany us to worship, educational, or fellowship events of our faith community. Such experiences not only sensitize families to the richness of others but also foster a deeper understanding of the spiritual dimension of family. Being in witness to homeless families, for example, allows us to see the truly spiritual center of life as well as the mutuality of sponsorship. Additional ways families can invite growth include reaching out to a family in crisis; involvement in social justice actions such as home renovation projects for the poor and elderly; inter-faith sharing/study groups; cross-cultural exchange programs; and co-owning a garden or large household item such as a lawn mower. Kathleen and James McGinnis, in *Parenting for Peace and Justice,* offer a multitude of possibilities for deepening our family life and values. The essence of their message is that the experience of living in a family should heighten our caring for life, strengthen our relationships with others, increase our self-growth, solidify our self-reliance, broaden our involvement in the faith community, enrich our understanding of spirituality, and support our growth toward vocation.

One important point about supporting family growth must be made. The daily arena of living offers young families many real problems to solve or cope with. Work demands, childcare problems, and conflicting family needs present many challenges to parents' faith in themselves and the goodness of the world in which they live. Faith communities must find ways to relate their worship, educational, and outreach offerings to the many reality issues confronted by parents. If young, poor, or single parents need a better support structure, they will not respond enthusiastically to an invitation to commit the next eight Tuesday evenings to a course on spiritual growth. Empowerment strategies we explored at Kanuga include sponsoring parent networks to reduce the sense of isolation many young parents feel; establishing family counseling and educational services on an inexpensive or sliding-fee scale; scheduling Parents Night Out childcare; assisting families to find and use those government services for which they are eligible; setting up a Lending Library for parents, and establishing an exchange service for children's outgrown toys and clothing. Parents should be surveyed to find what services *they* perceive are needed, and the orientation of such services should be toward building on strengths so that parents can enhance their image of themselves as capable of meeting the challenges of parenthood. We believe there is a strong, positive relationship between parents' self-esteem and willingness to envision a broader, richer image of themselves as persons, parents, and faith educators.

The foregoing pages offer many ways that faith communities can strengthen families for their faith journey, but we believe there is another crucial dimension which must be addressed. As advocates for persons in process, every faith community's mission must include influencing society toward a more just and compassionate design for valuing and supporting the growth of healthy families. Surely the best place to begin is in prayer that raises our spiritual awareness of the survival and growth needs parents and children must daily confront. We can, as we did at Kanuga , heighten our understanding of the realities many children experience—loneliness, confusion, abuse, and despair. These are seeds of more than unhappy lives; these are seeds of an eroding covenant. Such seeds need to be uprooted and replaced with nurturance of faith. This nurturance of faith begins with a recognition of our society's basic misappropriations of money, priorities, and valuing. The unfeeling, unsensing, and devaluing of life as a spiritual faith journey has been costly. The attitudes of "It's their child" or "I raised mine, you raise yours" are symbolic of social and spiritual need for renewal. A new vision of ourselves as being called into covenant to build faith communities of gentle, sensitive, and compassionate people is an essential starting point.

A second essential task is articulating the contributions which families and faith communities, working together as co-creators with God, make to each child's life-long faith development. Here we can enlighten community and business leaders about the complexities of family life, especially during the early years of family formation. If we believe that parents and infants form trust-bonds during the first months, parental leave policies must be designed so that young parents can retain job security, health care, and other benefits while taking time off from work to begin the family faith journey together in positive and sustaining ways. Where financial demands require parents placing young children with surrogate caregivers, we can advocate to improve the availability and quality of childcare and related family services, especially with regard to involving parents in the design, choice, and execution of these experiences.

Jim Fowler's presentation of the public church offers many ideas for strengthening the spiritual and temporal fabric in which families interact and grow. Whatever the mixture of stages and styles of faith, all our faith communities can educate within their context and beyond about the spiritual needs and gifts of families. All of us can pray in words and actions for a more just treatment of all families, and encourage a social justice emphasis in the activities of church committees and councils. And we can urge a new commitment to making children a part of our human and spiritual growth experiences.

The ministry of helping is rich with challenges throughout the family's lifespan. The strengthening of families is indeed a journey of trust that seeks to build a covenant of human justice and compassion. The Kanuga Symposium focused on the need for creating a faith community that nurtures this trust through faithful beginnings with families during their early years together. Our emphasis was on actions that can not only engage families in faith development but on strategies that might sponsor new beginnings of trust building in our communities. There were many hopeful signs that happened *at* Kanuga, but the most powerful ones are those which will happen *as a result of* Kanuga—a new vitality in our efforts to reshape what we and others are about on the journey of faith. In the words of Gertrud Mueller Nelson,

> Any contribution that we make to the fullness of time—to the creation of history—is finally a personal matter and draws on our efforts to fully become ourselves, each one of us in her or his unique life. Our personal self-realization also contributes to the universal community. Each of us, as we succeed or fail to call up into human consciousness the revelations that lie waiting for our transformation, contributes to or fails in the process that becomes the only way to change the course of human events and bring its healing (235).

6.

Inviting Children Into the Faith Community

Patricia J. Boone
Robert A. Boone

"Let us pray." With these words the faith community is called to worship. Adults, youth, and children are invited to participate in this act of worship. Week after week members of the congregation respond to the familiar phrase by bending their knees, closing their eyes, or bowing their heads. For many the call to prayer means we are about to talk to God, either on a personal or collective basis. But what does "Let us pray" mean to young children? Does their meaning resemble the meaning shared by the adult community?

A group of four and five year old children entered the church to explore the sanctuary. They were invited to blow out candles, wiggle their fingers in the water at the baptismal font, kneel on the kneelers, peer at the immense space of the room from behind the altar, talk through the public address system at the pulpit, make new sounds while punching those fascinating keys at the organ console, dress up in clergy stoles, taste a communion wafer, and sing a song in the choir pews. These sensory experiences enabled them to become familiar with the worship environment. This feast of holy bedlam concluded as the children gathered around the altar for a closing prayer. They were called to prayer with the familiar phrase, "Let us pray."

Back in the classroom, the children expressed some part of that experience at one of several activity centers. A young five year old wanted the group to see what he had made. Holding up his drawing, he asked us to guess what his picture was about. Not one of us guessed correctly. With great pride, the child pointed to the green-colored circle he had drawn and announced, "Why, this is lettuce pray!"

Children are keen observers, but their interpretations are not always accurate. While it is doubtful that adults would conjure up an image of a head of lettuce when called to prayer, this little boy made the best use of his imagination in making meaning of that phrase. And we wonder, what other interpretations, what other kinds of pictures are taking shape in this young lad's mind as he experiences the church? What is he learning about himself as a person and as a child of God? What sense is he making of the people around him and his relationships with them? Is this child learning anything about the use or misuse of power and authority which shape his life? What sense of purpose is emerging as this child moves through the stages of growth and development in his church community?

Parents, whether they are intentional about it or not, are the primary faith educators of children. But others in the faith community also influence the formation of attitudes which launch children into a lifelong journey of exploring the faith issues of *identity, community, authority*, and *purpose*. If we want our children to trust the loving God they cannot see, we have to provide a quality of life in the faith community where children experience trustworthiness and love.

Faith is a first-hand experience. It must be experienced before it can be shared. None of us can give away what we don't have. So it is unrealistic to expect any child to become a caring, giving adult if s/he has not experienced those faith qualities first-hand. Since faith attitudes are not automatically acquired at the time a child reaches maturity, we in the faith community have the opportunity to choose whether or not we will exercise our God-given responsibility to provide positive, first-hand experiences which influence the faith development of children in our congregations.

No child grows up faithless. Faith is learned in the context of relationships, and all children have relationships of some sort. It is through everyday experience with other people that young children learn what to think about themselves and how to value and interact with others. Children daily test their own sense of power in getting their needs met and their wishes fulfilled. They also come to know what it feels like when others exercise power and authority over them. Children begin to form impressions of usefulness and sense of purpose in these early years. All of these things are learned gradually in day-to-day experience. The key question is, where are young children getting their information?

The world of mass media is a rich source of information for children. Television, music, comic books and magazines, VCR tapes, billboard advertising, and the like provide a wide variety of answers to our faith questions about self, others, and the way to live life to the fullest. When the significant adults in a child's life model attitudes and qualities determined by the culture, is it any wonder that some children grow into a "secular faith"?

The world of childcare also provides information from which children synthesize emerging faith. How clearly do childcare workers recognize the degree to which their interactions influence a child's mental pictures of self and the world? Do church leaders, especially clergy, recognize the immense impact their childcare workers have on the faith development of young children? The faith community offers a great gift to children who live in the childcare world when it educates parents and caregivers to the fact that "earlier is better" refers to the teaching of positive faith attitudes more than it does to the teaching of reading in early childcare programs.

Children learn much from the world. To isolate them from it would do them a great disservice. After all, they will have to survive in this world one day as adult citizens making responsible choices. Whose worldview will they own by the time they become young adults?

The religious community has a wealth of resources to offer young children. These make it possible for children to formulate healthy attitudes about themselves and God's world. With regard to *identity,* the faith community can help children learn that they are more than consumers or competitors. They are unique persons accepted for who and whose they are rather than for what they will own or achieve some day. With regard to others, the faith community can enable children to discover that people in their world are trustworthy and respectable, others are not always to be feared, avoided, or manipulated.

Although children may learn through daily experience that money, status, and achievement bestow *power and authority,* the faith community can help them learn that power and authority are rooted in God's love for them and the world. Where today's society emphasizes that the *purpose* of life is to acquire wealth, achieve status, and maintain eternal youth, the faith community can help children acquire a deeper sense of purpose through learning to care for God's world and other people.

And so we see that children's day-to-day experiences shape the attitudes through which they will make meaning of their lives, attitudes which become the foundational building blocks for their faith development. The faith community has the opportunity to significantly influence this process as it welcomes young children into its worship, its story, its mission, and its hope.

Step One: A Place to Begin

The faith community is a kaleidoscope of personalities, interests, skills, and talents. The majority of adults are not likely to be experts in child development theory. But directly or indirectly, intentionally or unintentionally, adults influence children in their congregations. For those choosing to be intentional about it, where is the best place to begin thinking about positive ways to invite and influence children in the faith community?

Leaders in our congregation were discussing whether or not children should be in church. During a fascinating debate, one of them said children did not bother him, but he doubted they could learn anything by being in church. His supporters unanimously agreed. Later we invited him to think back to the earliest experience he could remember about church. Much to his surprise, his childhood memories danced their way into our conversation. For the next forty-five minutes this man relived sights, sounds, smells, frowns, glares, smiles, and warming glances of his early church experiences. He had not been in touch with the child part of himself in a long while. He concluded our conversation with, "Thanks. I needed that."

We all need that. God first encounters us through the child part of who we are. Any faith experience begins at this feeling level. The adult part of us seeks to make meaning of this experience and chooses to respond accordingly. In other words, throughout our lives we experience God through the child part of who we are, and we make meaning of that experience through the adult part of who we are. Many of our childhood attitudes and feelings stay with us and shape the channels through which we interpret our experience of God. In the Gospel of Mark, Jesus reminds us: "Truly, I say to you, whoever does not receive the Kingdom of God like a little child shall not enter it."

So adults wanting to be intentional about influencing the lives of young children might begin reflecting on their own experience. What was it like to be a young child in a faith community? One way for this to happen would be to provide adults of all ages the opportunity to share their early church related experiences with each other and to explore the impact their early years have had on their own faith journeys. Inviting adults to get in touch with the child part of themselves sensitizes them to the needs of children in their congregations. Exercises similar to these will heighten the congregation's awareness of what young children learn in the faith community.

Step Two: Clarifying Attitudes About Children

A young child in our congregation was struggling with her first aware-ness of death. She seemed preoccupied with the fear of losing her belong-ings. Her nightmares about loss and death intensified. The mother of this child, knowing that the child's deepest fear was her own safety, patiently approached the topic of death. In their discussion, it became apparent that the young girl worried about something dreadful happening to her mother and being left alone to take care of herself. The mother asked her daughter, "If something were to happen to me, if I were seriously injured, what could you do?" The child thought for a moment and said, "Well . . . I would call the people at the church."

The fact that this child thought of the church first suggests that the church community had become for her a second family, a group of people trustworthy and available to help. What made this so?

Many of us underestimate the degree to which children are attuned to our attitudes and feelings toward them. We assume that parents and the ever-faithful Church School teacher are the people in the faith community who influence children the most. While they do have a major impact on children, others of us, lay persons and clergy, can make a significant con-tribution to the children in our faith families. It is obvious that this young girl felt secure and loved because others in the church had been intentional in communicating to her that she was valued as a member of the congrega-tion, her faith family.

A logical next step in our efforts to welcome children into the life of the faith community, then, is for the adult members to examine and clarify their attitudes about children and how they are communicated. What "messages" are the children in our faith family receiving from us? Are they learning that we value in them what we want them to become some day? "Learn to behave in church, memorize the faith story and the community's guidelines for a moral lifestyle, explain the faith symbols and the nature of the sacramental life, and you, too, can become a person of faith when you grow up!" How easily we forget, especially when we don't have little ones in our homes, that children are more than empty minds waiting to be filled. They are spiritual persons overflowing with a rich sense of wonder and mystery, overflowing with a host of honest questions about life, the world, and God, overflowing with love to give and joy to share. Children have a natural thirst for faith. Do the faith community's attitudes about children squelch or quench this thirst?

Step Three: Responding With Respect

A third step for congregations to consider as they explore their relationships with children begins with the clarification of assumptions about how children learn and grow. While a Christian Education Committee struggled with the issues of children, church, and faith, they discovered the expectation for children to own their faith in the same sense that adults "own" faith. Children were expected to learn information about religion and apply it to their daily lives. The assumption was that faith equals the acquisition of information about religion. We are aware of one congregation where this assumption was the basis for their Sunday religious education program. Children were required to memorize information and pass written examinations on the material before they could move on to the next learning unit. Those children who could not pass the test made up the work during the summer. Some parents were pleased when their children excelled while other parents were embarrassed when their children did not perform as well. What a tragic mistake! Some children were learning to hate church while others were learning that salvation is achieved through good works. It is no wonder, as they "graduated" from Sunday School, that so many no longer wanted to come to church. An adult oriented approach to faith education is not appropriate for children. When we value most in children the adult we want them to become, we rob them of essential childhood experiences which are foundational to their faith development.

The Early Years

Fowler has shown clearly that faith is developmental. Just as a child's physical, social, and emotional growth develop in stages, so does his/her faith. As a congregation broadens its awareness of children's developing needs and abilities, it is better able to respond to children and incorporate them into the life of the community. How can a congregation respond to children's developmental needs?

Parents want children to respect their elders. God wants adults to respect his children. It is this mutual respect for one another and for God that binds us into community. Briefly, here are several ways a congregation can respect children and thereby influence their developing faith.

Infants and preschool children need, first of all, to feel safe. We respect this need and respond to it by providing appropriate space and responsible caregivers at those times when parents are involved in other congregational activities. To stash young children in the most convenient room available and to "get somebody to watch them" while we attend to our faith needs is disrespectful! The presentors at this Symposium have convinced us of the importance of trust in a young child's life. This need for a trustworthy environment and trustworthy caregiver does not stop at the church nursery door. As a congregation, we respect a child's emerging attitudes of self and the world when we provide a safe, stimulating room designed to meet needs and train caregivers to be sensitive to wants and fears. Young boys and girls can only learn to trust the God they cannot see through experiences which help them learn to trust the world they do see.

Second, young children have the need to learn about their world through exploration rather than through explanation. Many times we exclude children from worship and other church activities because they can't "understand" what is taking place. It is true that young children are unable to link pieces of information together to form a conclusion or arrive at a generalization. In this sense they don't understand, and, as we have seen, they often form misperceptions even though they are keen observers. But while adults are making meaning in abstract ways, young children are busy learning about the concrete world which we already know about and take for granted. A congregation respects children when we provide them opportunities to explore their synagogue or church through their senses. God is not offended by their curiosity or their fingerprints.

Third, young children need our patience and our praise. How many of us were raised under the assumption that we couldn't learn while wiggling? Our parents would not allow us to join them in a worship service until we could sit still and listen. Does God only love people when they sit still and listen? When the congregation respects a young child's need for wiggle time, we can exercise patience as this child learns to control impulses. Our patience helps children learn that their value as persons is a matter of who and whose they are rather than what they can or cannot do. Of course appropriate behavior is a legitimate learning goal for young children. We can support parents and teachers with this task as we turn from frowns and sighs of disgust toward praising children in their moments of appropriate behavior in our faith communities.

Fourth, young children are "either-or" learners. While it is important for parents and teachers to understand this, a congregation needs to know this too. Young children latch on to the images we give them and store them for future reference. They cannot absorb multiple images, especially contradictory ones. For example, it is a mistake to assume that children can simultaneously grasp the idea of a God who punishes and destroys, yet also loves. Some children will focus on images of a loving God while other children will focus on images of a God who punishes. Congregations and clergy respect children's needs for positive images as we are careful about the stories, pictures, and conversations we share with them. A parish hall or activity center adorned with portraits of stern-faced clergy of the past or with multiple images of a suffering God do little to teach young children that the faith community is a loving, caring, and trusting place! The images children form in their early years often become the images which surface during life crisis moments in adult life. In the hour of my greatest need, do I trust a God who loves, forgives, and accepts me or do I fear a God who punishes, scolds, and rejects me?

A fifth way congregations can respect preschool children is to recognize their need to learn through modeling the behaviors of others. A young mother expressed concern about her three young children who came to the Sunday dinner table in procession. The oldest child, holding a flashlight high above his head, led the way for the younger two children who were wearing toilet tissue stoles about their shoulders. "Lord, have mercy upon us, Lord, have mercy upon us, Lord, have mercy upon us," they chanted as they took their places at the table. The mother's anxiety about possible sacrilegious behavior peaked when the youngest child, using one of Mom's finest goblets, began serving communion to the members of her family. Of course the children were not being disrespectful. They were acting out what they had observed in church earlier in the day. They were trying-on-for-size these worship behaviors. The congregation respects this need to learn through modeling when we welcome young children into the various activities of community life. Exposing them to the movements and actions of faith, be they worship, education, or service to others, enriches their learning experience. Respecting their need to act out what they observe is a healthy way to reinforce their emerging attitudes about life in the community of faith.

On Beyond

Our children do not remain preschoolers forever. But they do carry with them the experiences, attitudes, and feelings rooted in this life phase as they journey into middle childhood, adolescence, adulthood, old age, and death. They will never lose the early childhood need to be cherished, nurtured, respected, accepted, and loved. However, the movement from early childhood to middle childhood brings with it additional abilities and learning needs which the faith community should consider in the effort to influence developing faith.

One sunny afternoon our daughter was seated on the patio gazing at the clear blue sky. When asked what she saw, Anna replied, "I don't think there really is a God or a heaven any more." Somewhat surprised by her six-year-old response, we asked why. She answered, "I have been looking up at the sky all afternoon, and I have not seen the bottom of the first foot."

Anna was moving from the preschool world of imagination into the middle childhood world of checking out what is real. The need to see the feet of saints and angels suggested that she was beginning to make sense of her world through literal interpretation and concrete expectations. Her brother, Jeremy, displayed the same need to sort out what is real from what is imagined. As a budding fifth grader, he questioned everything his parents attempted to explain. "Really, Dad?," or "That's not really true, Mom?" were frequent responses. What might have appeared on the surface as disrespectful behavior was, in fact, a developmental need in this child's life.

How is the faith community to respond to children in middle childhood? The need for proof frequently is displayed in the demand for fairness. In the child's mind, the people in his or her faith community are as real as they act. Adults volunteering to work with children at this stage in education classes, sports activities, church music programs, etc., need to know that children are placing "faith people" into clear-cut categories of mean or nice, glad or mad, like or dislike, fair or unfair. To expect grade-school children to see beyond our actions, or the lack of them, into our inner intentions is simply unrealistic. If we want these children to know that they are loved, cared for, and respected, we have to show it in ways which seem fair to them. They tend to see God in similar clear-cut categories and expect God to reward good behavior and punish bad behavior. And because these children are beginning to understand cause and effect relationships, they expect their communities to operate that way.

As children move into the early phases of middle childhood, a wonderful change takes place. For the first time they are beginning to pay attention to the ideas and perspectives of others. This enables them to form those important but shortlived best friendships and to develop their awareness of the need to belong. Congregations have the choice opportunity to influence children's emerging awareness of community, one of the four basic faith issues. Children have a need to be included in the life of the synagogue or church. How can clergy and congregations respond to this developmental need?

Exposing children to stories of the faith tradition and providing opportunities to tell and retell the stories in a variety of creative ways helps them claim a sense of ownership in the faith family. Remember, children love stories. At this stage they are developing the ability to remember them and to tell them because they can now recall the order of events in sequence and can better relate parts to the whole. Expecting boys and girls at this age to interpret the meaning of stories or to discern some moral truth between the lines is unrealistic. The meaning of stories for these children is trapped in the events as the tale unfolds. Because younger children at this stage have limited ability to understand concepts of time and history, they actually "live" stories in the present. Older children begin to develop an appreciation of "our people" from the past as they begin to grasp an understanding of time.

Congregations also influence children's developing sense of belonging in a variety of other ways. We can show appreciation when they display learning activities, remembering not to use adjectives which they may misinterpret as discounting or demeaning. Words like "cute," "sweet," "adorable," "precious," and "darling" sometimes communicate a belittling connotation.

We can include children in parish social events. They can be invited to help set tables, make placemats and centerpieces, serve food, and offer prayers of thanksgiving at covered dish suppers. The church can provide refreshments for children at coffee hours and have them serve as hosts and hostesses.

During the main worship service, have children bring Sunday School offerings to the altar as ushers bring forward the other congregational offerings. Invite children at this middle childhood stage to serve as ushers with their families or hand out service leaflets as the congregation gathers for worship. On special occasions, ask a group of children to design the leaflet or bulletin cover. In liturgical congregations, invite a group of children to observe and assist the altar guild for a month as they prepare the liturgical space for worship.

Encourage children to participate in clean-up activities around the buildings and grounds. They especially enjoy planning and maintaining a children's flower garden. Pride in their environment contributes to their pride in belonging to the congregation.

Outreach projects to the neighborhood or broader community provide a variety of opportunities to include children. Arrange for them to pack grocery bags with canned food at a community foodbank. Include them when painting outside walls of a house on a home improvement project. Arrange for them to clean up a leaf covered lawn for a homebound person on a rake-and-run cleanup project. Utilize their ideas and creative abilities in advertising posters for outreach projects of the congregation.

Children also enjoy intergenerational events where they can participate with adults of all ages in worship and learning. Creative play opportunities with parents and other adult members of the congregation quickly establish a sense of belonging for children.

The idea is not to have children take over traditional adult roles in the life of the congregation. But as we become more willing to share parish life events with them, they claim ownership and membership in the family of faith.

A Mutual Ministry

We have briefly sketched a procedure for congregations who want to be intentional about their influence on the developing faith of children. The three steps include: first, a reflection of our own experiences as young children and the impact these have had on our faith journey; second, an examination and clarification of the attitudes adults have about children in the congregation; and third, a demonstration of respect for our children through appropriate responses to their developmental needs and abilities as they grow through the stages of childhood in our faith communities.

Because faith develops within the context of relationships, this is a two-way process. It is a mutual ministry whereby children contribute to our emerging faith as we contribute to theirs. They bring to us a simple trust and an eager desire to enjoy the world and the people God has placed in their lives. Children are open to new experiences and welcome change as an opportunity for growth.   In our adult world of predict and control/prevent and repair, the presence of children reminds us that in the deepest sense, we, like them, come to God with a simple trust, an eagerness to grow in love, and an openness to wonder and mystery. To put it simply, without these childlike qualities our faith is reduced to religion.

7.

The Public Church: Ecology for Faith Education and Advocate for Children

James W. Fowler

When the planning committee for the Kanuga Symposium met in February of 1987, we found ourselves, toward the end of our work, asking the following questions:

(1) What kind of church or religious community is capable of providing the sort of nurturing for infants and children that we envision from this conference?

(2) What kind of church is capable of calling and forming adults to be the kind of persons who can be advocates for children, not just within the church, as important as that is, but in the larger society and political process as well?

In response to those questions I introduced the concept of the "public church." As we discussed this vision of the church, the planners asked me to develop a presentation to relate the developmental stages of selfhood and faith to the tasks, mission, and character of a public church, especially as it advocates for children. This chapter represents my effort to meet that request.

What is the "public church" and why is the idea potentially important here? Stop and reflect for a moment on the meaning of the term "public" as an adjective. For many persons, associations with the modifier "public" are not particularly positive: public transportation, public restrooms, public housing, and the like. Acknowledging the ambivalence that surrounds the term, let me give you a bit of background on why the idea of the public church has emerged as a very important one in my view. Sociologist Daniel Bell, in a book called *The Cultural Contradictions of Capitalism,* gave a trenchant look at the effects of modernity, the effects of post-industrial living, on American life. He said that if we look at our lives and society carefully, we see that they are divided into three separate or disjunctive spheres.

Bell suggests that much of our life is lived in the sphere he calls the "techno-economic order." This is the order in which we work and make a living, the order in which we contribute to the economy. He points out how powerful the techno-economic order can be in our family lives and in our personal lives. It can move us around the country; it can literally move us around the world, if we will let it, and want badly enough to reap its rewards. The techno-economic order as an order of work has its own ethical codes. It has its own structure of values. It becomes one of the important contexts in which our fundamental worldviews and attitudes are profoundly shaped or changed.

The techno-economic order, for many of us, is separated from our participation in another important sphere of life, which Bell calls "polity" or "governance." All of us are citizens. And yet, Bell observes, more and more the work of governance is being done by professional elites. It is harder and harder for private citizens to say, "I need to take a year or two out from my work and run for Congress." To mount a successful campaign, there are PACs that must be lined up for financial support; vast amounts of money must be accumulated for political consultants and television campaigns. Running for a governorship requires a minimum of two million dollars in most states for the media and the mounting of the campaign. Polity, therefore, has become a separate sphere with its own professional standards, its own world of significance and meaning, and its own professional elite. The participation of average citizens is more and more that of spectators being entertained in their living rooms.

Then Bell points to our participation in a third sphere which he calls "culture." By culture he means all of those dimensions of our lives where we have private time, discretionary time, and where we can use the money we have left over from the struggle for survival. This is the world of the family, of friendship, the arts, of volunteer service, of sports and leisure, and the like. It is interesting to note that Bell puts religion squarely in the middle of this privatized dimension that he calls culture. He claims that religion and other traditional sources of ethics and normative standards no longer have much impact in the more public worlds of the techno-economic order and the order of the polity. Culture becomes more and more a matter of privatized meanings and relations, in which we associate with persons very much like ourselves. Our gathering may give us encouragement and support, but it makes very little impact on our participation in the techno-economic and political orders. This is the disjunction of spheres of our lives.

Around the middle of the 1970's, we began to see the emergence of what the media came to call the new religious right. We began to see the emergence of the "Moral Majority" and many other such groups. In part, the Moral Majority and related organizations of the new religious right formed in order to try to address the disjunction of spheres that Daniel Bell identified. Religionists on the right insist that religion *must* have some impact on the ways we make our livings. Religion *must* have an impact on government; religion *must* have an impact on public education. One might wish that the Moral Majority had been as stringent in looking at the standards and ethics of the techno-economic order as it tried to be in looking at the governmental order. Any Marxist would likely tell us that there is a fair amount of false consciousness involved in the failure to take on the ethical vacuum in much of business and corporate life. But that's not my major point. I'm leading up to saying that the so-called mainline denominations have also been deeply affected by the disjunction of spheres. We need to be involved in making our own serious efforts to re-knit work, citizenship, family, and faith. This mending of the divided spheres is crucially important if we are asking what kind of adults can become advocates for children in our world today. We must become churches that take account of and try to impact the techno-economic order and the political order as well as the more private order of culture—family, religion, and education.

The Idea of a Public Church

Let me present a distillation of six principal qualities of the public church. First, it is a church that is deeply and particularly Christian. We are not advocating here some sort of religion in general or a bland, homogenized brand of ecclesial life. In this respect and others, the public church is to be clearly distinguished from the idea of an American civil religion. Rather, we have in view congregations which have a spine of identity, grounded in their convictions of the truth of the gospel. They are worshiping communities whose life is centered in God's self-revelation in Jesus Christ. They are praying, praising, and proclaiming communities. They may be Protestant or Catholic, Orthodox or Evangelical. I believe there are or can be equivalents to the public church in Jewish, Muslim, Buddhist, and other religious communities. In these pages, however, I will deal with the Christian instance. The public church is deeply and particularly Christian.

Second, as churches committed to Jesus Christ, under the sovereignty of God, public congregations are prepared to pursue their missions in the context of a pluralistic society. Such churches acknowledge religious pluralism, not so much as a burden to be tolerated, but as a condition to be affirmed and engaged. They do not believe that the only faithful way to relate to their variety of Christian and non-Christian neighbors is through proselytization, on the one hand, or anathema or judgment, on the other. Such churches are prepared to give their witness and to invite the stranger to saving faith in Jesus Christ. But they are also willing to share their story and offer the wisdom of the Christian faith to others in a spirit that intends relation and cooperation for the common good.

The ability to relate non-defensively to persons and groups of other or of no religious backgrounds arises out of an openness that is born of identity and conviction. My colleague Walter Lowe once reminded us that openness is a second level virtue. Often openness is spoken of as though it were a primary virtue, like faith, hope, love, or courage. But it is not; it is derivative. When you have only openness, you don't have much. A window stuck *open* is as bad as a window stuck shut; in either case you have lost the use of the window. Openness is a second level attribute of a system or organism that has significant structure and integrity in itself. Openness is possible for persons or communities who know who they are. When the spine of identity is well established, it is possible to risk relating in depth to those who are different from the self. The public church exhibits a principled openness, in the midst of pluralism, born of its clarity about its convictional grounding and corporate identity.

Third, churches that have identities grounded in conviction can be churches committed to civility. Civility involves effective commitment to the kind of discourse and engagement in public that allows us to express deep convictions, address controversial concerns, and differ with others profoundly, without having either to decimate the opponent or to withdraw from the encounter. Such churches are committed to trying to restore public space, space where discussion about the issues that matter on the human agenda can be addressed in fullness and in depth. Jesuit philosopher Walter Ong reminds us of the original meaning of the term "campus." Originally a campus was a field of combat where people engaged in struggle, but without resort to weapons. Public churches are committed to joining with others to create campuses where the stranger can be met humanely and where we can struggle over issues that matter, without resort to violence. The public church is committed to sponsoring and practicing civility.

Fourth, public churches are those in which the encouragement of intimacy within the community and the concern for a family-like connectedness are balanced by care about the more impersonal and structural domains of public life. In fact, without a healthy measure of pluralism within the community, allowing conflict and struggle between people who have significant differences among them, the church will not prepare people for robust witness and service in their public vocations. Public churches encourage and support their members in the development of vocations in which partnership with God is carried into the large-scale economic, technical, political, commercial, and religious structures that shape our lives. Public churches try to free their members from many of the tasks of institutional maintenance and internal ministry for the sake of strengthening their vocations as Christians in the marketplace, the school, the law office, the legislative halls, the hospitals, and the corridors and committees of peace-making. Public churches call forth and empower lay ministry, not by telling lay women and men what they should do in the contexts of the complex systems in which they live but by giving them access to and grounding in scriptures and tradition so that they can become informed practical theologians and ethicists in their roles as leaders and followers in their lives in public.

Fifth, public churches try to offer their witness and vision in a public language. Offering Christian witness and vision in public language means trying specifically to address people from the standpoint of our tradition and the Gospel in ways that can be understood beyond the circles of those who have been socialized into the unique language and symbols of our particular traditions. In their two letters on nuclear disarmament and the national economy, the American Catholic bishops gave us examples of a great church trying to do public theology. In their introductions to the nation, they indicated first that they were concerned with the pastoral task of trying to form the consciences of Catholic Christians. In those two letters, however, they went on to say that their research and consultations had gone beyond the Bible and ethical traditions of the church. They had made serious efforts to offer their arguments and proposals with a kind of rationality that would call forth dialogue with all interested Americans who might read or discuss the documents.

Finally, public churches are unafraid of engagement with the complexities and ambiguities of thought and ideologies in this age of ideological pluralism. Convinced of the sovereignty of God, public churches know that God is greater and more than even our most adequate theologies can fully grasp. Therefore such churches engage with others in a non-defensive openness, guided by the confidence that God often uses the truths of others to refine, reground, or correct our own. They witness to the transcendent God whose self-disclosure is the center of our history—the hinge of history—and who keeps coming to us from the future, expanding and correcting our grasp of the event of Christ and giving us eyes to see and nerve to respond to the in-breaking kingdom of God.

An Interliving Ecology of Faith Consciousness

Now let us look at the public church as an ecology for faith education. Here we will refer to Figure I, which gives you a kind of diagrammatic representation of the seven stages of faith that our earlier research has yielded.

I call your attention to the circular placement of the symbols of these stages of faith, hoping it will suggest to you a quality of interliving across stages. By arranging the stages in this circular pattern, I want to flesh out the idea that a public church ought not to be a place where we struggle for a homogeneous unity or to get everyone to conform to one modal level of faith development. Rather it is a community which, within itself, is a kind of celebration of unity and pluralism. The church ought to be a place where, as Peggy Way once said, we come to learn to stand each other. This means understanding ourselves as a covenant community, a community called into being by God, and not a community that initiates its own identity through a contractual process. As a covenant community, called from beyond ourselves into being, we realize that it doesn't matter too much whether we really like each other or not, at least at the beginning. We are there for other reasons than warm compatibility, and in the rubbing against each other and the supporting of each other we engage in the process of being formed into something that God can use in God's world,

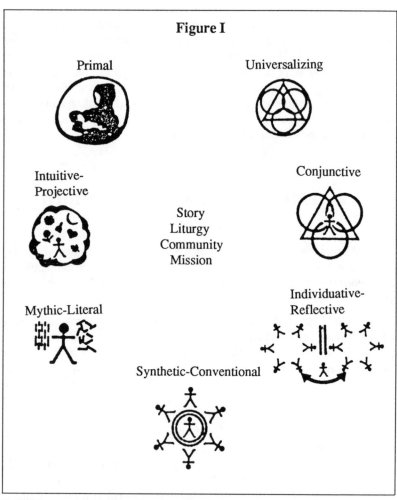

Figure I

Primal

Universalizing

Intuitive-
Projective

Conjunctive

Story
Liturgy
Community
Mission

Mythic-Literal

Individuative-
Reflective

Synthetic-Conventional

in covenant partnership. That's what I want to suggest with this circular patterning of the symbols of the stages of faith.

Notice at the center that this covenant community is held together by its shared story and stories. How do we form a spine of identity? We remem-

ber, tell, and enact our stories. I saw this graphically illustrated by an old
Jewish friend of mine, Sam Buchlaender. Stocky and bald, with a com-
manding presence, Sam was born about 1900 in Russia, the son of a
wealthy Jewish lumberman. His father had what Sam called *Privaszittlesvodt,* a kind of special license that Jewish merchants were required to have
by the Czar in order to operate in Moscow. But that *Privaszittlesvodt*
didn't keep his wife from being cut down by a cossack's sword in view of
her children in the pogrom of 1905. In 1912 his father gave to Sam two insurance policies, one guaranteed by Czar Nicholas II and the other by
Kaiser Willhelm of Germany—great security in the coming world! Sam
had made and lost more fortunes than any other person I have known. He
had accumulated and lost more libraries than anyone I have known. But he
also studied with Rabbi Jacob Klausner at Yeshiva Slobadka in Odessa,
Russia, where he learned to interpret the Talmud and Midrash.

When I knew Sam, he was sitting on Heider Mountain in western North
Carolina. He was, as a common friend of ours said, a manic depressive.
This friend went on to say, however, that Sam wouldn't be normal, given
the life he'd had, if he wasn't somewhat manic depressive. It was Sam
who taught me about the importance of stories and the spine of identity.
Had he not had a spine of identity, after the way life had pushed him
around, he would not have known who he was in his old age. Sam had the
disconcerting habit of thinking in terms of millennia. He watched to discern what the Holy One was doing over centuries. Therefore he was not so
disturbed about what might happen today or tomorrow; he knew there was
a bigger story going on.

The question is, how do we ground ourselves in a spine of identity that
holds us together in this covenantal living? Look for the centripetal pulls
inside the circle in Figure I. We call the story *kerygma;* we call it Gospel.
It is the narrative vantage point, given through the Bible and the Christ, on
what God is doing in this world. It calls and informs us for being part of it.
Then we're held together by liturgy, *leiturgia,* the "work of the people." In
the sacraments and worship, through the work of physical and interactional
meaning-making and meaning-celebrating, we re-enact our story in our
corporate lives. We are held together and formed emotionally and morally
by our liturgies. Further, we are held together by community, *koinonia.*

We are held together by that quality of interpersonal faithfulness, of knowing and supporting each other, that church, at its best, offers in an unparalleled way. On some days the Christ wears the human face of someone who makes God's love real and present to us. And, finally, we're held together by our service and mission, by our *diakonia*. This includes our common and our separate vocations to be part of the purposes of God in the world. It includes our partnership in God's creative work, God's governing work, God's liberating and redemptive work in the world.

Now who are these folk who are being held together in a public church? Who are these people who represent different stages and ways of being in faith? Let's look briefly at these different, interliving stages of faith. (Fowler, *Stages of Faith; Becoming Adult; Pastoral Care*). In Figure I we see at the top left the image that represents a Madonna-like figure and an infant, and we recall in that symbol all that we said earlier about mirroring, about the eyes that recognize and the face that blesses. We see all that we said about the child's recruitment of the parent through his or her own capacities for smiling, responding, and initiating relationship. Here we are in the arena of *primal* faith, in which we form, as awkward as the word may sound, our *pre-images of faith*. Images are very important things in our lives; they hold together our affect, our deep feelings about something, and what we know, with whatever degree of clarity, about it. Pre-images are those pre-conscious clusters of knowing and feeling which constitute the rudiments of our sense of faith in others, faith in the self, and faith in God.

Then we have those in the congregation who represent the remarkable *intuitive-projective* stage of faith. The diagram shows us a child, awakening to almost daily novelty and newness in his or her growth and experience of the world. Such a child hasn't yet established logical operations by which to sort out, name, and order the world. But her imagination is flourishing, and she forms deep-going and long-lasting images of her experience of the world, of others, and of whatever lies beyond. In this stage a child dependably will encounter the reality of death, either in the death of a pet, a relative, or the relative of a friend. At or around four years of age, the reality of death breaks upon us, and then we ask, "Who will take care of me if those I depend upon should die? What will happen to me if I die?

Where do we go beyond death?" The question of that penumbra of mystery that surrounds our life invites the child to imagine and to explore in a reverent and often very private kind of mysticism. We know that the child's imagination and spirit, his capacities for forming a meaningful world, can be exploited by communities that too early convince him of his badness and press the fact that he must be "saved" in order to alleviate that innate badness. You can ensure that a child will have a conversion experience by age eight if you fill him with enough imagery of the threat of hell and of his badness. We know that we can exploit the religious imagination of the intuitive-projective child. But we also know that we can gift it with images by which children can grow toward Godliness and toward fuller humanity.

This brings us to the stage of the *mythic-literal* way of being in faith. The mythic-literal is the stage of the school child, the child who experiences the awakening of the capacity for narrative. The child is ready not only to hear and repeat stories, but to tell stories and to conserve meanings in and through narratives. The child wants to know the stories of "our people" and the stories that illumine what it means to be part of our family. My wife, Lurline, and I were visiting with her brother, who has an adopted son. He was about eight, and the father, a very busy surgeon, did not have a lot of time to spend in telling the boy stories of his family. Lurline, using the time visitors sometimes have that parents don't, began to tell about the boy's adopted father's boyhood and some of the things that happened in those earlier years. I watched from a distance. I could almost see the boy growing physically and his back straightening as he got the stories that enabled him to tie into his family in ways that he had not had access to before. Narratives of belonging. Still at the concrete level, we do not do abstract reflection in this stage. But we do form a sense of identity grounded in the stories of our tradition.

The next stage brings us to the *synthetic-conventional* members of the community, typically beginning around early adolescence and continuing for a time. This stage is made up of those who begin to discover in a new way their own interiority and the depths of the interiority of others. This is the stage in which we learn to construct the perspectives of others upon our selves, to see ourselves as we think others see us. And pretty soon we realize that others see themselves as they think we see them, and we understand why St. Augustine, writing about this period of his life, would say, "And I became a problem to myself." The diagram shows us a person standing within a circle of significant others, being mirrored in new ways. The mirroring enables the person of selfhood to form a set of beliefs, values, and attitudes that can sustain the forming sense of identity as s/he takes a place in a community of *con-forming* others. We must remember, also, that there can be many adults in the congregation who are best described by the synthetic-conventional stage of faith. Such adults rely upon the approval and authority of external or internalized others. They prize warmth and closeness in the congregation and are deeply concerned when conflict threatens to arise. They may be disturbed at the call to unity in diversity espoused by the public church.

Sometime in young adulthood or later we see for many people the emergence of what we have called the *individuative-reflective* stage of faith. Here we see the self, no longer sustained by and embedded in its roles and relationships as in the synthetic-conventional stage, but facing the question, "Who am I when I'm not defined by my roles and relations, by being so-and-so's son or daughter or so-and-so's spouse? Who am I when I'm not defined by my relationship to those people who matter most to me? Who am I when I'm not defined by my roles in the world of work? Is there an 'I' that has these roles and relations but is not fully expressed in any of them?" And we see that person asking a new set of questions about his/her beliefs or values. "What is it that is true and authentic for me? What beliefs and standards are congruent with the self I feel myself most clearly to be? To what ideology or worldview can I be committed with integrity? And what groups does that mean I need to be loyal to?" These are issues for individuative-reflective faith. That stage can carry adults a long way.

Around midlife, thirty-five or beyond, we see some people who seem to have undergone another revolution in faith, a revolution toward a stage that we call *conjunctive* faith. In the chart you see a self at the point of intersection of several circles of meaning and relation. What the previous stage worked so hard to gain clarity about, in terms of the boundaries of the self and the structure of beliefs and values, the conjunctive stage seems to have to allow to become more complex. The person begins to come to terms with the fact that there is a deeper part of the self, an unconscious self, that also controls his/her behavior and reactions. If one has specialized in being male or female, s/he may have to come to terms with the fact that contra-sexual (opposite sexual) qualities are also part of the self and must be integrated into one's way of being a man or a woman. The polarities of being both young and old must be taken into the self. Moreover, such persons may find themselves saying with St. Paul, "The good I would do, I do not do. The evil I would not do, I find myself doing. Who will save me from this body of death?" The conjunctive stage brings the paradoxical unity of opposites within us.

In the diagram those circles also represent the self's recognition that we live in the midst of systems, and that systems have to be dealt with in our social experience. Religiously, it means that we are aware of the depths of the God reality in new ways. It may become a matter of interest and importance that God has many names. Such persons may recognize that God has a shadow side and a hidden side, and may begin to recognize that just as we never know another human being fully, we certainly will never know God in full. A kind of epistemological humility becomes an important part of faith. Also important for our consideration of the public church is the fact that persons of the conjunctive stage exhibit a principled openness to the religious truths of others and have a readiness to relate with receptivity to persons and groups of other religious and ideological traditions. This is not wishy-washy openness, but the openness I wrote about earlier in this chapter, born of deep convictions and a clear spine of identity.

Exemplified by a few persons in congregations we may see the stage that we call *universalizing* faith. In the diagram you notice that the human figure has disappeared. This does not mean that persons described at this stage cease to be human, in every sense of that word, or that they totally cease being self-concerned. But it does mean that there seems to be a kind of shift, a regrounding of the self and its valuing and knowing, toward a grounding in the transcendent or the Beyond. In my limited experience of them, these persons seem to love in a way that participates more fully in God's love than the rest of us. They seem to love their enemies and those who would slay them with a kind of self-abandon, even as God might love those persons.

In this brief overview of stages of faith I have invited you to view the congregation as an ecology of faith consciousness. It is an ecology of different styles and ways of being in faith. Jerome Berryman has coined a term, "cross-stage static," that helps us understand some of the difficulties we have in the kind of congregation that really cultivates this interliving of stages. When people go at the business of being Christian or being faithful in different stages, what matters to them in the tradition will also differ. Cross-stage static is always a reality within a community and beyond a community.

Let me move now to questions about nurture in faith development and the modal developmental level found in a public church. What do I mean by "modal developmental level"? A mode is a kind of average. The modal developmental level of a group is the average expected level of development for adults within that community. If a community of faith is very large and diverse, it may be a multi-modal community. If so, it will sponsor people to different adult levels, and it will keep a quality of openness that will nurture them in ongoing growth. For a church to be a public church, and to have the qualities that I spelled out in the first part of this chapter, there must be strong segments of the congregation at both the individuative-reflective and the conjunctive stages. This means we're looking at an inter-generational church in the full sense of the word. We are looking at a church that makes a place for children, for parent, and for grandparent generations. It must sponsor both generational interliving and appropriate ongoing development in faith for each group.

The Public Church as Ecology for Faith Education

Let's look briefly at each of these major phases from infancy up to the early school years and think together about how a public church tries to nurture formation in faith. We've said a great deal about the need in infancy for mutuality and faithfulness—"trustworthiness" as Betty Caldwell called it. I call it "proto-covenantal faithfulness"—the kind of faithfulness that is prior to the explicit embrace of covenantal living. As regards proto-covenantal living, which is the quality of mutuality that invites infants to selfhood and faith, we need to see the church as providing "holding environments." In German the term is *Spielraum,* a "play space," a safe place for the dangerous work of becoming a self and forming faith. Such a play space needs to combine freedom and support, limits and permission. And it requires trustworthy adults who have faithful fantasies and visions for children, as well as a healthy regard and love for the child as he or she is. Such a community needs to provide ritual and stories rich enough to form the emotions of children. Faith, hope, and love are emotions in the deep sense of being profound dispositions and virtues, the orienting strengths of personhood. The church can provide rituals and stories sturdy enough to form the emotions and shape virtues.

The work of George Lindbeck, in a book called *The Nature of Doctrine,* helps us begin to see how this deep structure of faith and confidence works in our lives. He says that the deep structure of Christian faith is like the deep structure of language. We try to capture the deep structure of language through the rules of grammar. But you don't learn the rules of grammar until long after you've become a speaker of the language. We need doctrine as rules of faith living, once we've already been formed in the deep structure that makes us Christian folk. A tradition that has that quality of depth forms in us the dispositional pattern that it is in loving and being loved that we find the full measure of self-realization.

In churches which practice infant baptism, preparation for the welcoming and the baptism of the child in the Christian community should begin before birth. Parents should be helped to understand that the foundations of faith—the pre-images of God, self, and world—begin to form certainly at birth, and likely before birth, during intro-uterine experience. As they anticipate the baptism of a newborn, family members can be helped to reflect on and clarify their own understandings and practices of faith. What kind of faith do they want to nurture this child in? From the beginning the baby, before reflective consciousness and language have been acquired, embarks on the venture of composing a sense of the family's patterns of faith. Parents and other family members convey their trust and their loyalties, their priorities and commitments, through the everyday ritualization and interactions of family life.

Let's look at the intuitive-projective stage of faith in early childhood for a moment. Here our opportunity and our calling is to try to gift the imaginations of children and to form habits of virtue (Fowler, *Gifting the Imagination*). For young children I want to stress approaches to the Bible which put them into the stories as physical, feeling or emotional, as well as thinking and interpreting, participants (Furnish, *Exploring the Bible*). Informed by Stern's work, we have new understandings of how this kind of approach takes account of the core self of the child in the experience of sharing and making meaning. As an example, let us take the parable of the Good Samaritan. Let us imagine that one of the four year olds has been invited to play the role of the wounded person, and s/he adopts the position of the wounded person on the floor. Now what is that child experiencing with his/her body on that floor? S/he is experiencing hurt and helplessness, exploitation and degradation. When we invite a couple of children to be the priest and the Levite, what physical experiences do they have as they walk by and see this helpless other, and feel their feet drawing them in another direction, avoiding the pain, hurt and humiliation? Then we invite another child to play the compassionate Samaritan. What physical experience does s/he have of tactile contact with, and material help to, the prone and suffering wounded person? In that process, as we allow other children to play each of those parts, we find that at the level of the core or body self they feel the impact and shaping power of the story.

What do they experience at the level of the subjective self—the level of feelings and taking the perspectives of the feelings of others? When they concretely play the different roles, the children are able to penetrate what it feels like to be in each of those positions. Finally, when we talk about the experience and tell the story again, we're addressing the level of the verbal self and its meanings. After the experiencing of the other two levels, children are enabled to speak with a greater meaning and authority about this parable. And, as Berryman has rightly warned us, we keep the meanings of those stories open-ended and fluid so that the child, having these gifts to the imagination, can continue to grow toward new levels of understanding.

Corresponding to the importance of putting children in Biblical stories is their sacramental involvement and participation (Browning and Reed). Where infant baptism is understood as the rite of entrance into the church, it is important to invite young children to experience involvement in the baptismal service, as well as to participate in the eucharistic celebration. (We will have to work out different understandings of how young children are welcomed into the people of God in congregations where believers' baptism is practiced.) Such participation is essential because, again, it addresses those three pre-verbal levels of the self, long before the child will understand or be able to articulate the meaning of the sacraments. It provides them with the physical experiences of kneeling and of being in the midst of the community of faith and the sensory experiences of tasting the wine and bread. These represent formative experiences of faith and solidarity. The subjective meanings of faith will gradually grow as the child explores and talks about the feelings that s/he has in these experiences. Then at a later stage, when s/he is ready, the theological foundations that have been experienced can be brought to word and doctrine.

The stories that are enacted in worship and sacrament give us a profound cluster of forming elements. Stories give us the sources of our identity, our origins, our nature, our destiny as persons and as a people. Stories give us models of character, examples to follow, and examples to avoid. Stories give us indications of the nature and the disposition of God. They show us God's suffering and pain and God's compassion. Stories give us indications of the way life is and of the disciplines that are required to live it well, with courage and resourcefulness. Janice Hale-Benson, in her presentation at the Symposium, was profound when she pointed to the danger of giving our children only victory stories and victory expectations. She helped us see the tremendous importance of teaching them that life can be hard, it can be difficult, and it requires solidarity with others. Life requires courage and determination; it requires virtue and will, suffering and joy.

Let us turn now to a consideration of faith formation for school age children, at the stage that we call mythic-literal faith. I've been very impressed with an approach to worship readiness which my wife, Lurline, has developed in our own congregation. Over a period of six years, she and her children's council have intentionally worked to include and involve children in the rather large and formal Sunday worship in the Glenn Memorial Church. From ages four to nine, these children participate with their parents in the first half of the service. They leave after the offertory and just before the sermon. The preschoolers retire to supervised play and refreshments; those from ages six to nine go in the fall weeks to a class in worship readiness. Over a period of twelve weeks, they become familiar with all of the movements and the elements of the weekly liturgy. They learn about hymns and creeds and different forms of prayer, about paraments and stoles and the seasons of the church year. They enact and experience chances to try leadership in the different aspects of the liturgy; they learn about the lectionary and the challenge of preaching from the texts. I went there one Sunday after they had been studying the church year and one little girl—a third grader who had been through this several times—explained to me about the lectionary and gave me a little disquisition on the preacher and his challenge to preach something fresh from those texts every week. I got the impression that she was awakening to the possibility that she might like to take on that challenge, and she felt that she might well have something to say!

Special care is taken in introducing the sacraments. The Biblical stories and the sources for baptism and the eucharist are shared. The difficult issues of crucifixion and resurrection are addressed sensitively but head-on. The children have a chance to make bread for the Eucharist and to present at the time of offering. On two occasions recently elementary classes have stood as sponsors with families who are presenting their infants for baptism because the parents of the babies had been the children's teachers, and they were able to anticipate the baby's coming through the period of the pregnancy. It does not matter that our children repeat this introductory orientation to and involvement in the liturgy and the sacraments at least three times. It comes, as we have discovered, at exactly the right time for them, a time when their interest in the dramatic and the symbolic dimensions of worship are at a peak and when their newly emerging capacities for grasping the narrative dimensions of the Christian tradition give great impetus and enthusiasm to their learning the stories of faith. With each repetition they capture new dimensions and depth, and the older children begin to teach the younger ones in a very interesting and impressive way.

The Public Church as Advocate for Children

In conclusion, let me lift up several important considerations for a public church that wants to be an advocate for children. First, there's advocacy on behalf of families. Families provide for four important ontic needs that children and adults universally require. Although families come in many shapes and forms, all families need to be supported in providing four elemental kinds of experiences. First, families are meant to provide the experience of communion and valued place for children. All that we've said about physical care, all that we've said about affective attunement, all that we've said about the telling of stories that tell us who we are and give us a sense of belonging comes into play here. All play key roles in providing experiences of intimacy and in conveying to the child a sense of irreplaceability. None of us is indispensable, we like to say, but all of us need somewhere to be irreplaceable. We need to be cherished for who we are and what we are and to know that we belong in a profoundly valued way. Families provide that, and public churches need to support families in providing that cluster of experiences.

Second, families provide children with experiences of agency and responsible autonomy. We need, under safe conditions, to learn gradually that we can make a difference in our own lives and in the lives of others. We need to learn that we can be agents in our own existence, in responsible autonomy. The family is the place where we step out upon the stage for the first time, to be autonomous actors. (I'm using "stage" now in a different sense from the one I've used previously, though the double meaning is interesting.) Here we find out the kind of roles we can play by the responses we elicit from that first audience, our family. The family needs support in providing for children experiences of autonomy, agency, and responsibility.

Third, a family needs to provide shared meanings and rituals. Life in the home offers the child's first experience of being part of a social construction of reality. Families need support in working out the sharing of meanings and rituals, the use of language, and the telling of stories. Children need the everyday informal rituals as well as more formal ones; churches can guide and empower families in this kind of understanding.

Finally, families need to provide shelter and nurturance, food and care, and opportunities for sexual identification. Ideally, each young child would have access to parental figures of both sexes during the crucial period from birth to age five. We are having our attention called now to a syndrome that seems to be particular to boys between the ages of eighteen and thirty-six months which psychiatrists are calling "father hunger." This term refers to the boys' emotional and physical need for consistent interaction with a parent or parent-surrogate who is a dependable, available, loving male figure. For the boy, engaged in making that dangerous process of first separation from his deep attachment to the first loved object, the mother, this seems to be profoundly important. It is a crucial time for forming gender identification with a male. In church schools where fathers are teaching nursery classes, we see boys who have no available father figure gravitate quickly to the male figures in their class environment.

Notice that I gave you these ontic needs that families meet not in a hierarchy like Maslow's hierarchy of needs but in a circle of needs that have to be met at every stage if there is to be being and well-being. In this circle of ontic needs, the provision of food and basic care can be sacramental. We convey our sense of the irreplaceability of the other in the way we carry out those rituals of basic provision.

Let me now mention a second important area of advocacy for children. We need to help families and the children that we care for in nursery school, daycare, kindergarten, or Sunday School classes, avoid the hurrying and miseducation to which David Elkind has so forcefully called our attention in his writings. His most recent book, *Miseducation,* builds upon the earlier, *The Hurried Child.* It especially alerts us to the dangers of those policies and public pressures on legislatures and state boards of education to press full-day kindergarten back into the four year old level and to carry elements of the curriculum of the first grade back into kindergarten. My objection, here, is not to the provision of quality childcare for three and four year olds on an all day basis. Rather, following Elkind and Piaget, I believe that we must resist the precocious forcing of the learning of reading, writing, and arithmetic skills upon children before they are developmentally ready and to the detriment of very important social learning and play prior to and during the fifth year. Such policies can be disastrous and lead to severe school "burnout" by the time a child reaches middle school. As of this writing, there are twenty-four states where legislation is already on the boards to extend kindergarten and first grade curriculum downward into the fourth and fifth years. We need to speak out against this pressure while supporting and working for quality childcare.

In closing, I must try to evoke and focus our awareness of the biggest challenge advocates for children face in our present society and world. As I undertake to do this, I want to flash back for a moment to another era and to circumstances that must have seemed then as threatening as do those we face today. The time, mid-eighteenth century; the place, England. As we walk the streets of certain districts of London we see drunks sprawling in filthy gutters. We see dirty-faced, hungry children begging or stealing money and scraps of food. We see women and children probing garbage bins and homeless immigrants from rural areas sleeping at night wherever they can. Men can be hung for stealing a loaf of bread to feed their families or poaching a deer from an aristocrat's fields; and hangings, conducted in open squares in the city, are the chief form of public entertainment. On Sunday afternoons solid burghers roll prostitutes down hills in barrels for sport, while during the week children work from pre-dawn darkness to darkness again in filthy sweat shops.

This is the England of John Wesley. The evangelical revival which he led, and which began the Methodist movement, generated the will, the vision, and the energy to address the urban and rural degradation of persons in Wesley's day. We in our time, however, face conditions in our major cities that would make even a Wesley blanch. Carol Rodning, a member of the Kanuga Symposium, is a researcher in early child development in Los Angeles. She and her colleagues are studying children, the majority of whom have a parent involved in substance abuse. In many instances the parents are young teenagers themselves. Her description of these children's circumstances forces us to face the degree to which infants are experiencing insult at each of the points of emergent selfhood and faith I wrote about in my earlier chapter of this book. Impaired in many instances by drug dependence acquired through the mother, and frequently impaired by birth defects due to poor prenatal care, vast numbers of children are consigned to minimal, arbitrary, and inconsistent adult care. Cared for by street-wise older siblings and the ubiquitous television, they miss out on many of the crucial experiences of affect attunement, bonding, and symbol and language acquisition. Carol's words are chilling as she describes children, who, over the first three or four years of life, steadily manifest an erosion of developmental potentials. "It is as though a light within them begins to dim and go out," Carol said, "and after a point, I doubt whether, in most cases, it can ever be lit again."

Carol and her colleagues work with one hospital (only one of six in that part of the city) where some ten thousand babies, most in similar circumstances, are born each year. Her work is replicated in virtually every other major American city. While thirteen percent of all Americans today live beneath the federal poverty level, more than twenty percent of all American children live in poverty conditions. Where drugs, alcohol, prostitution, and the economy of the streets prevail, children have harsh struggles for survival. In what epitomizes my vision of hell, the structures of fidelity, of care, of humanizing bonds and attachments have largely broken down and a ghastly contemporary version of Hobbes' war of all against all has emerged. A public church must face the fact that our nation and its government have largely broken faith with our fellow citizens who live in these circumstances. Such conditions constitute a mirror for us of the underside of our social, political, and economic systems. They mirror to us the underside of our individualism in religion and of our intoxication with our own efforts at survival, security, and flourishing.

Of course, through government agencies we pour considerable amounts of money into support of the urban poor, and there are heroic teams of social workers and urban advocates ministering among them. Carol Rodning has pointed to the irony that in many instances tax monies are used to purchase drugs and maintain addictions as well as to support detoxification and rehabilitation efforts. These conditions in our cities call for more. A John Wesley would have rolled up his sleeves. Can we, as members of public churches roll up ours?

How do we generate the will, the compassion, the focused outrage, and vision that can engage the terrible challenge of our cities and their insult to children? Walter Brueggemann has written about what ancient Israel did when the dehumanizing experiences of enslavement and oppression became too much to bear. They undertook what he calls the "public processing of pain." So long as the abject misery of persons in our inner cities is insulated from view and concern, we, as churches and as a society, will not address the range of fundamental issues which must be addressed. Such a public processing of pain has already begun with marches and documentaries on the plight of the homeless. We must do more of that, focusing upon the overcrowded location centers in old urban hotels being provided as housing for mothers and children. Aside from the general effects of poverty, those environments provide virtually no protection from the exploitative energies of the pushers and the pimps.

While churches alone cannot solve the multi-layered problems that dehumanize persons and put children at risk in our cities, we can play crucial catalytic and inspiriting roles. This is a time for demonstration projects of reclamation and prevention. This is a time for the renewal of an inclusive social covenant. This is a time for the public processing of pain and of possible solutions. As members of public churches we may have resources of hope and imagination not available to our secular counterparts. At least we *should* have.

If we do not address this demonic dehumanization going on in our cities, if we allow it to continue, we in our nation will yield to a decline that will make the decline of Rome and other great civilizations look like a sunset over against apocalypse. We cannot let God's children continue to be treated like trash, and turned into trash.

I want to conclude with something from *The Book of Common Prayer* (828-9) written in an earlier time, as a kind of benediction for the children and families of our world:

Almighty God, our heavenly Father, who settest the solitary in families: We commend to thy continual care the homes in which thy people dwell. Put far from them, we beseech thee, every root of bitterness, the desire of vainglory, and the pride of life. Fill them with faith, virtue, knowledge, temperance, patience, godliness. Knit together in constant affection those who, in holy wedlock, have been made one flesh. Turn the hearts of the parents to the children, and the hearts of the children to the parents; and so enkindle fervent charity among us all, that we may evermore be kindly affectioned one to another; through Jesus Christ our Lord.

AMEN.

References

Introduction

Berryman, Jerome. "Being in Parables with Children." *Religious Education* 74 (1979): 271-85.

Brophy, Beth et al. "Children Under Stress." *U.S. News and World Report* 27 October 1986: 58-63.

Children's Defense Fund. *A Call for Action to Make our Nation Safe for Children: A Briefing Book on the Status of American Children in 1988.* Washington: Children's Defense Fund, 1988.

Edelman, Marian Wright. *Families in Peril: An Agenda for Social Change.* Cambridge, MA: Harvard University Press, 1987.

Elkind, David. *The Hurried Child: Growing Up Too Fast Too Soon.* Reading, MA: Addison-Wesley, 1981.

_____. *Miseducation: Preschoolers at Risk.* New York: Knopf, 1987.

_____. "The Role of Play in Religious Education." *Religious Education* 75 (1980): 282-93.

Episcopal Church. *The Book of Common Prayer.* New York: Church Hymnal Corporation and Seabury, 1977.

Forliti, John E., and Peter L. Benson. "Young Adolescents: A National Study." *Religious Education* 81 (1986): 199-224.

Gallup, George, Jr. Introduction. "Key Battles Being Won in War Against Alcohol Abuse and Alcoholism." *Alcohol: Use and Abuse in America.* Gallup Report No. 265. Princeton, NJ: The Gallup Poll, 1987.

The Gallup Poll. *Religion in America.* Report No. 259. Princeton, NJ: The Gallup Poll, 1987.

Gore, Tipper. *Raising PG Kids in an X-Rated Society.* Nashville: Abingdon, 1987.

Goldman, Ronald. *Readiness for Religion: A Basis for Developmental Religious Education*. London: Routledge and Kegan Paul, 1965.

Harris, Maria. "A Model for Aesthetic Education." *Aesthetic Dimensions of Religious Education*. Ed. Gloria Durka and Joanmarie Smith. New York: Paulist, 1979, 141-52.

Langway, Lynn et al. "Bringing Up Superbaby." *Newsweek* 28 March 1983: 62-8.

Magid, Ken, and Carole A. McKelvey. *High Risk: Children Without A Conscience*. Golden, CO: M & M Publishers, 1987. Reprinted New York: Bantam, 1988.

Peck, M. Scot. *People of the Lie*. New York: Simon, 1983.

Postman, Neil. *The Disappearance of Childhood*. New York: Delacorte, 1982.

Robinson, Haddon. "More Religion, Less Impact." *Christianity Today*, 17 January 1986: 4-5.

Sawin, Margaret. "Family Enrichment—The Challenge Which Unites Us." *Religious Education* 75 (1980): 342-53.

"A Special Call to Act." *Ecumenical Child Care Newsletter*, May-June 1987: 5.

Strommen, Merton P., and A. Irene Strommen. *Five Cries of Parents*. San Francisco: Harper, 1985.

Werner, Emmy E. "Resilient Children." *Young Children* 39.7 (1984): 68-72.

Westerhoff, John H. *Will Our Children Have Faith?* New York: Seabury, 1976.

Chapter 1: Strength for the Journey

Berryman, Jerome. "Being in Parables with Children." *Religious Education* 74 (1979): 271-85.

_____. Public Dialogue. Institute of Religion, Houston, TX, 1976.

Brueggeman, Walter. *Hope Within History*. Atlanta, GA: John Knox, 1987.

Erikson, Erik H. *Childhood and Society*. 2nd ed. New York: Norton, 1963.

_____. *The Life Cycle Completed*. New York: Norton, 1982.

_____. *Toys and Reasons: Stages in the Ritualization of Experience*. New York: Norton, 1977.

_____. *Young Man Luther: A Study in Psychoanalysis and History*. New York: Norton, 1962.

_____. *A Way of Looking at Things*. Ed. Stephen Schlein. New York: Norton, 1987.

Fowler, James W. *Faith Development and Pastoral Care*. Philadelphia: Fortress, 1987.

_____. "Gifting the Imagination: Awakening and Informing Children's Faith." *Review and Expositor* 80.2 (1983): 189-200.

_____. *Stages of Faith: The Psychology of Human Development and the Quest for Meaning*. San Francisco: Harper, 1981.

Fowler, Jim, and Sam Keen. *Life-Maps: Conversations on the Journey of Faith*. Ed. Jerome Berryman. 2nd ed. Waco, TX: Word, 1985.

Hart, Ray L. *Unfinished Man and the Imagination*. New York: Herder, 1968.

Hillman, James. *Re-Visioning Psychology*. San Francisco: Harper, 1975.

Mahler, Margaret, Fred Pine, and Anni Bergman. *The Psychological Birth of the Human Infant*. New York: Basic, 1975.

Messer, Alfred. "Father Hunger." *Journal of the Medical Association of Georgia* 74 (1985): 822-4.

Miller, Alice. *Thou Shalt Not Be Aware: Society's Betrayal of the Child*. New York: Farrar, 1984.

Moseley, Rommey M., and Ken Brockenbrough. "Faith Development in the Preschool Years." *Handbook of Preschool Religious Education*. Ed. Donald Ratcliff. Birmingham, AL: Religious Education Press. In press.

Ong, Walter J., S.J. *The Presence of the Word*. New Haven, CT: Yale University Press, 1967. The thought is found in pages 198-201.

Osmer, Richard, and James W. Fowler. "Childhood and Adolescence— A Faith Development Perspective." *Clinical Handbook of Pastoral Counseling*. Ed. Robert J. Wicks, Richard D. Parsons, and Donald E. Capps. Mahwah, NJ: Paulist, 1985.

Piaget, Jean. *The Child and Reality*. New York: Penguin, 1979.

_____. "Piaget's Theory." *Carmichael's Manual of Child Psychology*. Ed. Paul Mussen. 3rd ed. 2 vols. New York: Wiley, 1970, pp. 703-32.

_____. *Play, Dreams and Imitation in Childhood*. New York: Norton, 1962.

Piaget, Jean, and Barbel Inhelder. *The Psychology of the Child*. New York: Basic, 1969.

Polanyi, Michael. *The Tacit Dimension*. Garden City, NY: Doubleday, 1967.

Rizzuto, Ana-Maria. *The Birth of the Living God: A Psychoanalytic Study*. Chicago: University of Chicago Press, 1981.

Stern, Daniel. *The Interpersonal World of the Infant: A View from Psychoanalysis and Developmental Psychology*. New York: Basic, 1985.

Way, Peggy. Public lecture. Candler School of Theology. Emory University, Atlanta, GA, 1981.

Winnicott, Donald W. *Playing and Reality*. New York: Basic, 1971.

Chapter 2: Roots of Faith

Ainsworth, Mary D. "Early Caregiving and Later Patterns of Attachment." *Birth, Interaction, and Attachment*. Ed. Marshall H. Klaus and Martha O. Robertson. Skilman, NJ: Johnson and Johnson, 1982.

Bandura, Albert. "Social Learning Theory of Identificatory Processes." *Handbook of Socialization Theory and Research*. Ed. David A. Goslin. Chicago: Rand, 1969.

Baumrind, Diana. "Some Thoughts about Child Rearing." *Child Development: Contemporary Perspectives*. Ed. Stewart Cohen and Thomas J. Comiskey. Itasca, IL: F.E. Peacock, 1977.

_____. "New Directions in Socialization Research." *American Psychologist* 35 (1980): 639-52.

Bradley, Robert H., and Bettye M. Caldwell. "The HOME Inventory and Family Demographics." *Developmental Psychology* 20 (1984): 315-20.

Bretherton, Inge. "Attachment Theory: Retrospect and Prospect." Bretherton and Waters, 3-35.

Bretherton, Inge, and Everette E. Waters, eds. "Growing Points of Attachment Theory and Research." *Monographs of the Society for Research in Child Development* 50 (1, 2, Serial No. 209) 1985.

Briggs, Dorothy. *Your Child's Self-Esteem*. Garden City, NY: Doubleday, 1975.

Children's Defense Fund. *A Children's Defense Budget FY 1988: An Analysis of our Nation's Investment in Children*. Washington: Children's Defense Fund, 1987.

Coles, Robert. "The Faith of Children." *Sojourners*, May 1982: 12-16.

Erikson, Erik H. *Childhood and Society*. New York: Norton, 1950.

_____. "The Father of the Identity Crisis." *Growing and Changing: What the Experts Say*. Ed. Elizabeth Hall. New York: Random, 1987.

Fraiberg, Selma. *Clinical Studies in Infant Mental Health: The First Year of Life*. New York: Basic, 1980.

George, Carol, and Mary Main. "Social Interactions of Young Abused Children." *Child Development* 50.2 (1979): 306-18.

Gilligan, Carole. *In A Different Voice*. Cambridge, MA: Harvard University Press, 1982.

Heschel, Abraham J. *God in Search of Man: A Philosophy of Judaism.* New York: Jewish Publication Society of America, 1955.

Honig, Alice S. "The Art of Talking to a Baby." *Working Mother* 8.3 (1985): 72-8.

_____. "The Eriksonian Approach: Infant/Toddler Education." *Approaches to Early Childhood Education*. Ed. Jainpual L. Roopnarine and James E. Johnson. Columbus, OH: Merrill, 1987.

_____. "The Gifts of Families: Caring, Courage, and Competence." *Family Strengths 4: Positive Support Systems*. Ed. Nick Stinnet et al. Lincoln: University of Nebraska Press, 1982, pp. 331-50.

_____. "High Quality Infant/Toddler Care: Issues and Dilemmas." *Young Children* 41.1 (1985): 41-6.

_____. "Training of Infant Care Providers to Provide Loving, Learning Experiences for Babies." *Dimensions* 6.3 (1978): 33- 43.

_____. "What are the Needs of Infants?" *Young Children* 37.5 (1981): 3-10.

Honig, Alice S., and Donna S. Wittmer. "Teacher-Toddler Day Care Interactions: Where, What, How?" *Stimulation and Intervention in Infant Development*. Ed. David Tamir et al. Jerusalem: Freund Pubs., 1985.

Kaplan, Louise J. *Oneness and Separateness: From Infant to Individual*. New York: Simon & Schuster, 1978.

Kegan, Robert. *The Evolving Self: Problem and Process in Human Development*. Cambridge, MA: Harvard University Press, 1982.

Kohlberg, Lawrence. *Child Psychology and Childhood Education*. White Plains, NY: Longman, 1987.

Kushner, Harold S. *When Children Ask About God*. New York: Shocken, 1976.

Lickona, Thomas. *Raising Good Children: From Birth Through the Teenage Years.* New York: Bantam, 1983.

Martin, John A. "A Longitudinal Study of the Consequences of Early Mother-Infant Interaction: A Microanalytic Approach." *Monographs of the Society for Research in Child Development* 46 (3, Serial No. 190), 1981.

Matas, Leah, Richard Arend, and L. Alan Sroufe. "Continuity of Adaptation in the Second Year: The Relationship between Quality of Attachment and Later Competence." *Child Development* 49.3 (1978): 547-56.

Piaget, Jean. "Piaget's Theory." *Carmichael's Manual of Child Psychology.* Ed. Paul Mussen. 3rd ed. 2 vols. New York: Wiley, 1970, 703-32.

Pines, Maya. "Good Samaritans at Age Two?" *Psychology Today* 13.11 (1979): 66-74.

Ricks, Michael H. "The Social Transmission of Parental Behavior: Attachment across Generations." Bretherton and Waters, 111-27.

Sears, Robert L. "Identification as a Form of Behavioral Development." *The Concept of Development.* Ed. Dale B. Harris. Minneapolis: University of Minnesota Press, 1957.

Segal, Julius, and Zelda Segal. "Talking about God." *Parents* 62.9 (1987):208.

Stern, Daniel N. *The Interpersonal World of the Infant: A View from Psychoanalysis and Developmental Psychology.* New York: Basic, 1985.

Vaughn, Brian E., Kathleen E. Deane, and Everett Waters. "The Impact of Out-of-Home Care on Child-Mother Attachment Quality: Another Look at Some Enduring Questions." Bertherton and Waters, 110-35.

Chapter 3: A Faltering Trust

Bradley, Robert H. "Play Materials and Intellectual Development." *Play Interactions: The Role of Toys and Parental Involvement in Children's Development.* Ed. Catherine C. Brown and Allen W. Gottfried. Skilman, NJ: Johnson and Johnson, 1985, pp. 129-42.

Bryan, James H., and Perry London. "Altruistic Behavior by Children." *Psychological Bulletin* 73.3 (1970): 200-11.

_____. "Preaching and Practicing Generosity: Children's Actions and Reactions." *Child Development* 41 (1970): 329-53.

Bryant, William Cullen. "Thanatopsis." *Poems for Youth: An American Anthology.* Ed. William Rose Benet. New York: Dutton, 1925, p. 10.

Dinkmeyer, Don. "Top Priority: Understanding Self and Others." *Elementary School Journal* 72.11 (1971): 62-71.

Elardo, Phyllis T., and Mark Cooper. *Aware: Activities for Social Development.* Menlo Park, CA: Addison-Wesley, 1977.

Elardo, Richard, and Bettye M. Caldwell. "The Effects of an Experimental Social Development Program on Children in the Middle Childhood Period." *Psychology in the Schools* 16.1 (1979): 93-100.

Erikson, Erik H. *Childhood and Society.* New York: Norton, 1950.

Friedrich-Cofer, Lynette K. et al. "Environmental Enhancement of Prosocial Television Content: Effects on Interpersonal Behavior, Imaginative Play, and Self-Regulation in a Natural Setting." *Developmental Psychology* 15 (1979): 637-46.

Gelles, Richard J. Address. "A Profile of Violence towards Children in the United States." Annenberg School of Communications Conference on Child Abuse: Cultural Roots and Policy Options. Philadelphia, PA: November, 1978.

Guidubaldi, John et al. "The Impact of Parental Divorce on Children: Report of the Nationwide NASP Study." *School Psychology Review* 12 (1983): 300-23.

Hoffman, Stevie, and Becky Wundram. "Sharing is . . . ." *Childhood Education* 60.4 (1984): 261-5.

Honig, Alice S. "Prosocial Development in Children." *Young Children* 37.5 (1982): 51-62.

Kessen, William. *Childhood in China.* New Haven, CT: Yale University Press 1975.

Kritchevsky, Sybil, Elizabeth Prescott, and Lee Walling. *Planning Enivronments for Young Children: Physical Space.* Washington: National Association for the Education of Young Children, 1969.

Levitt, Mary J. et al. "Reciprocity of Exchange in Toddler Sharing Behavior." *Developmental Psychology* 21.1 (1985): 122-3.

Martorella, Peter H. "Selected Early Childhood Affective Learning Programs: An Analysis of Theories, Structure, and Consistency." *Young Children* 30.4 (1975): 289-301.

Montagu, Ashley. "Friendship-Loving: What Early Childhood Education is All About." *Connecting: Friendship in the Lives of Young Children and Their Teachers.* Ed. D. Palmer Wolf. Redmond, WA: Exchange Press, 1986.

Moore, Shirley G. "The Unique Contribution of Peers to Socialization in Early Childhood." *Theory into Practice* 20.2 (1981): 105-8.

Rogers, Carl. *On Becoming a Person: A Therapist's View of Psychotherapy.* Boston: Houghton-Mifflin, 1961.

Shure, Myrna B. "Social Competence as a Problem Solving Skill." *Social Competence.* Ed. Jeri D. Wine and Marti D. Smye. New York: Guilford, 1981, pp. 158-85.

Shure, Myrna B., and George Spivack. "Interpersonal Cognitve Problem-Solving and Primary Prevention: Programming for Preschool and Kindergarten Children." *Journal of Clinical Child Psychology* 2.11 (1979): 89-94.

_____. "Interpersonal Problem-Solving as a Mediator of Behavioral Adjustment in Preschool and Kindergarten Children." *Journal of Applied Developmental Psychology* 1.1 (1980): 29-43.

_____. "The Problem-Solving Approach to Adjustment: A Competency-Building Model of Primary Prevention." *Human Services* 1.1 (1981): 87-103.

_____. *Problem-Solving Techniques in Childrearing.* San Francisco: Jossey-Bass, 1978.

Spivack, George, and Myrna B. Shure. *Social Adjustment of Young Children.* San Francisco: Jossey-Bass, 1974.

Stern, Daniel. *The Interpersonal World of the Infant: A View from Psychoanalysis and Developmental Psychology.* New York: Basic, 1985.

Teasdale, Sara. "Barter." *Love Songs.* New York: Macmillan, 1927, p. 3.

Yarrow, Marian R., Phyllis M. Scott, and Carolyn A. Waxler. "Learning Concern for Others." *Developmental Psychology* 8.2 (1973): 240-60.

Chapter 4: Attitude Education in Early Childhood Faith Development

Barber, Lucie W. Presidential Address. "Proactive Religious Education." Annual Meeting, APRRE. Anaheim, CA: Nov. 18-22, 1983.

_____. *The Religious Education of Preschool Children.* Birmingham, AL: Religious Education Press, 1981.

_____. *When A Story Would Help.* St. Meinrad, IN: Abbey Press, 1981.

Barber, Lucie W., and John H. Peatling. *A Manual for the Barber Scales of Self-Regard: Preschool Form.* Schnectady, NY: Character Research Press, 1977.

_____. *Realistic Parenting.* In collaboration with Sr. Marie Skoch and Rev. John T. Hiltz. St. Meinrad, IN: Abbey Press, 1980.

Blazer, Doris A. "The Influence of Parental Participation in a Parent Education Program upon the Self-Concepts of Preschool Children." Dissertation. University of South Carolina, 1981.

Bugelski, Bergen R. *The Psychology of Learning Applied to Teaching.* New York: Bobbs-Merrill, 1964, p. 38.

Cooney, Ellen W., and Robert L. Selman. "Children's Use of Social Conceptions: Toward a Dynamic Model of Social Cognition." *New Directions for Child Development.* Ed. William Damon. San Francisco: Jossey-Bass, 1978.

English, Horace B., and Ava C. English. *A Comprehensive Dictionary of Psychological and Psychoanalytical Terms.* New York: McKay, 1962.

Erikson, Erik H. *Identity and the Life Cycle.* New York: Norton, 1980.

Hampson, Ann. "Pre-Kindergarten Attitude Education." *Character Potential: A Record of Research* 6.2 (1973): 112-20.

Hilgard, Ernest R. *Introduction to Psychology.* New York: Harcourt, 1962, p. 631.

Lee, James Michael. *The Content of Religious Instruction.* Birmingham, AL: Religious Education Press, 1985.

_____. *The Flow of Religious Education: A Social Sciences Approach.* Birmingham, AL: Religious Education Press.

Little, Sara. *To Set One's Heart: Belief and Teaching in the Church.* Atlanta, GA: John Knox Press, 1983.

Rambo, Brenda C. "A Comparative Study of Children's Self-Concept in Two Preschool Programs as Measured by Child, Mother, and Teacher." Dissertation. George Peabody College of Teachers of Vanderbilt University, 1982.

Westerhoff, John H. *Bringing Up Children in the Christian Faith.* Minneapolis, MN: Winston, 1980.

Williams, Herman, and Ella Greene. *Attitude Education: A Research Curriculum.* Schnectady, NY: Character Research Press, 1975.

Zeldin, Michael. "Jewish Schools and American Society." *Religious Education* 78.2 (1983): 182-92.

Chapter 5: Strengthening Families

Burchard, John, and Sara Burchard. *Prevention of Delinquent Behavior.* Newbury Park, CA: Sage, 1987.

Fowler, James. "Faith and the Structure of Meaning." *Toward Moral and Religious Maturity.* Ed. James Fowler and Antoine Vergote. Morristown, NJ: Silver Burdett, 1980.

_____. *Stages of Faith: The Psychology of Human Development and the Quest for Meaning.* San Francisco: Harper, 1981.

Galinsky, Ellen. *The Six Stages of Parenthood.* Reading, MA: Addison-Wesley, 1987.

Magid, Ken, and Carole McKelvey. *High Risk: Children Without a Conscience.* New York: Bantam, 1987.

McGinnis, Kathleen, and James McGinnis. *Parenting for Peace and Justice.* Maryknoll, NY: Orbis Books, 1985.

Nelson, Gertrud M. *To Dance with God.* New York: Paulist, 1986.

Pittman, Frank. *Turning Points: Treating Families in Transition and Crisis.* New York: Norton, 1987.

Spivack, George, and Nancy Cianci. "High-Risk Early Behavior Patterns and Later Delinquency." *Prevention of Delinquent Behavior.* Ed. John Burchard and Sara Burchard. Newbury Park, CA: Sage, 1987.

Westerhoff, John H. *Bringing Up Children in the Christian Faith.* Minneapolis, MN: Winston, 1980.

Chapter 6: Inviting Children Into the Faith Community

It would be impossible to list all the resources shared by Kanuga Symposium participants. Here are some which will expand the ideas presented in this chapter.

Barber, Lucie W., *The Religious Education of Preschool Children* (Birmingham: Religious Education Press, 1981). We first learned of attitude education through this book. Seven foundational attitudes are described with practical recommendations for teaching them to young children in several phases of early childhood development.

Detrick, Ralph L., and Mary Cline Detrick, *Christian Community* (Atlanta: John Knox Press, 1981). This is a good program for congregations who are planning an intergenerational program for the first time. Supplemental activities for children six and under need to be added if this age group is to be included.

Fowler, James W., *Faith Development and Pastoral Care* (Philadelphia: Fortress Press, 1987). This book provides a very helpful summary of the stages of faith development and selfhood. Chapter five, "The Congregation: Varieties of Presence in Selfhood and Faith," offers suggestions for interacting with children in both Intuitive-Projective and Mythic-Literal faith stages.

Lickona, Thomas, *Raising Good Children* (New York: Bantam Books, 1982). Based on the work of Lawrence Kohlberg, this book offers a method of parenting within the framework of moral reasoning development. It includes a clear description of each developmental stage beginning with infancy. Practical strategies for helping children to grow within each stage are clearly defined.

Ng, David, and Virginia Thomas, *Children in the Worshiping Community* (Atlanta: John Knox Press, 1981). This book explores the problems and possibilities of including children in congregational worship. Parents and clergy will learn a variety of techniques for teaching children about worship. The last chapter, "How a Pastor Relates to the Children," provides ideas worthy of clergy consideration.

Nouwen, Henry J.M., *Reaching Out* (Garden City, New York: Doubleday, 1975). Of the three movements of the spiritual life, the second from hostility to hospitality, requires our making space for the guest. In the chapter "Forms of Hospitality," helpful insights into the relationships between parents and children, teachers and learners, and patients and healers challenge us to rethink the relationships between children and congregations.

Westerhoff, John H., "The Church and The Family," *Religious Education* 28, 2 (Spring, 1983): 249-71. In this article a distinction is made between the cultural family and the faith family. The faith family is described as a type of community with common memory, common vision, common authority, and common ritual. In the faith family, congregations are to do things *with* families rather than *for* families.

Chapter 7: The Public Church

Bell, Daniel. *The Cultural Contradictions of Capitalism.* New York: Basic, 1976.

Browning, Robert L., and Roy A. Reed. *The Sacraments in Religious Education and Liturgy.* Birmingham, AL: Religious Education Press, 1985.

Episcopal Church. *The Book of Common Prayer.* New York: Church Hymnal Corporation and Seabury, 1977, p. 829.

Elkind, David. *The Hurried Child.* Reading, MA: Addison-Wesley, 1981.

_____. *Miseducation: Preschoolers at Risk.* New York: Knopf, 1987.

Fowler, James, W. *Becoming Adult, Becoming Christian.* San Fancisco: Harper, 1984.

_____. *Faith Development and Pastoral Care.* Philadelphia: Fortress, 1975.

_____. "Gifting the Imagination: Awakening and Informing Children's Faith." *Review and Expositor* 80.2 (1983): 189-200.

_____. *Stages of Faith: The Psychology of Human Development and the Quest for Meaning.* San Francisco: Harper, 1981.

Furnish, Dorothy J. *Exploring the Bible with Children.* Nashville: Abingdon, 1975.

_____. *Living the Bible with Children.* Nashville, Abingdon, 1979.

Lindbeck, George A. *The Nature of Doctrine: Religion and Theology in a Postliberal Age.* Philadelphia: Westminster, 1984.

Marty, Martin E. *The Public Church.* New York: Crossroad, 1981.

Palmer, Parker J. *The Company of Strangers.* New York: Crossroad, 1981.

Roozen, David A., William McKinney, and Jackson W. Carroll. *Varieties of Religious Presence: Mission in Public Life.* New York: Pilgrim Press, 1984.

Stern, Daniel. *The Interpersonal World of the Infant: A View from Psychoanalysis and Developmental Psychology.* New York: Basic, 1985.

Appendix: Staff and Steering Committee Members

Kanuga Symposium on Faith Development in Early Childhood

The Rev. Robert A. Boone
Associate Rector, St. Christopher's Church
Pensacola, Florida
Past Chairman, Christian Education Commission
    (Episcopal) Gulf Coast Diocese

Dr. Doris A. Blazer
Associate Professor, Early Childhood Education
    Furman University
Greenville, South Carolina
Coordinator, Kanuga Preschool/ Parenting Conferences

Dr. Kathryn Chapman
Associate Professor, Childhood Education
Southern Baptist Theological Seminary
Louisville, Kentucky

Ms. Carolyn Deitering
Church of the Sacred Heart (Roman Catholic)
Tucson, Arizona
Parish Liturgist and Free-lance Liturgical Dancer

Ms. Margery Freeman
New Orleans United Methodist Urban Ministries
    Childcare Programs
New Orleans, Louisiana
Field Associate, Ecumenical Child Care Network

Ms. Ann Gordon
Executive Director, National Association of Episcopal Schools
New York, New York
Formerly Lead Teacher, Bing Laboratory School,
    University of Southern California

Ms. Rose Helms
AAMFT-Certified Family Therapist
Swansboro, North Carolina
Formerly with Project Enlightenment
    Raleigh, North Carolina

The Rev. Dr. John T. Hiltz
Parish Priest, St. Martin D'Poores Church
Yorba Linda, California
Formerly Director of Religious Education
    (Roman Catholic) Diocese of Toledo, Ohio

Ms. Sandra Holloway
Lutheran World Federation
Geneva, Switzerland
Formerly Director for Childhood Ministries
    American Lutheran Church,
    Minneapolis, Minnesota

Dr. Jean Floyd Love
Minister to Children
Covenant Presbyterian Church
Charlotte, North Carolina
CE:SA Early Childhood Curriculum Writer

Ms. June Rogers
Bangkok, Thailand
Formerly Director, Child Advocacy Office
    National Council of Churches of Christ, New York

Dr. Kevin Swick
Professor, Early Childhood Education and
    Director, Children's Center,
University of South Carolina
Columbia, South Carolina
Past President, Southern Association on Children Under Six

The Rev. Leonard (Bud) Wilmot
Department of Ministry with Children
American Baptist Churches
Valley Forge, Pennsylvania